Where Are Your Accusers?

Words Matter Because You Matter

BETTY RUSSELL

✳

This is such a powerful book, and a delightful guide, full of important information for those of us who want to enjoy a face-to-face encounter with Jesus, walking free from sin consciousness and guilt.

*[Loaded with the MSB
(Mirror Study Bible)]*

Thank you, Betty Russell, for this excellent work.

Francois du Toit
Author of the *Mirror Study Bible*

DEDICATION

To my Beloved husband, Lloyd
Thank you for choosing me.
Thank you for treating me as a vessel of honor,
and cherished treasure, from the moment we spoke
our first words to one another.
Thank you for trusting me with your heart, while you so gently yet
tightly held onto mine, unconditionally.
You encouraged me when I gave in to discouragement.
You believed I could, when I lost sight of the goal.
TWO truly became better than ONE.
"I LOVE YOU MORE."
YOU WILL FOREVER BE MY ALWAYS.

To my 6 Treasured Children,
Rebecca, Priscilla, Sabrina, Andrea, James, and Joey
Thank you for sharing your life with me and allowing me to share mine
with you. In the uniqueness of each one of YOU,
I have seen by example what it looks like
to choose
light over darkness, joy over sorrow,
forgiveness over bitterness,
life over death, love over fear.
Thank you for the LIGHT, JOY, FORGIVENESS, LIFE
and LOVE
you have shown me so UNCONDITIONALLY.
You are truly gifts from the Lord, once carried in my womb
and forever always in my heart

To my precious Puppy, "Teddy"
You were created by God to Instinctually love UNCONDITIONALLY.
Thank you for your slobbery kisses, your anticipated joy upon my
arrival from being away 5 minutes or 24 hours. Thank you for allowing
me to snuggle with you when I needed it more than you did.
You are a precious gift.

ENDORSEMENT

The greatest gift God has given to me in this lifetime is my precious wife, Betty. Our journey began in 2015. Within a 24 hour period of time, Spirit opened Betty's and my eyes to the truth of Christ in all people. It has been such a wonderful blessing to passionately travel together this road to understanding God's unconditional love. Betty calls this experience her "Road to Emmaus". I refer to it as, "Once I was blind, but now I can see."

We had both been raised in Fundamental Evangelical teachings. I am thankful for this upbringing because it was all part of the journey. I believe I would not have discovered the TRUTH, had I not first been exposed to doctrines of men.

There is one incident I will always remember as standing out the most in our journey. Spirit used one of these doctrines of men to begin the process of removing the scales from our eyes. The little church we had been attending for about 4 years then, had planned a Baptismal ceremony. We were all gathered on the banks of the Rogue River to celebrate a young man, Andy, who had made a decision to follow Jesus. This was particularly special for us because Andy had lived in our home for about a year. The three elders in our church stood together in the River with him. One of them addressed the crowd with this question. "Did Jesus die for everyone?" Out of my mouth, from the heart, I shouted, "YES!" Within seconds, a voice from behind us spoke these shocking words which I will never forget. "No He didn't."

From that moment we began to sense a stirring in our hearts. Spirit began to open our eyes to God's unconditional love for ALL mankind. This TRUTH stood in stark contrast to the lie proclaimed that day on the River's edge.

There are no conditions in unconditional Love.

"There is only one God. He remains the ultimate Father of the universe. We are because He is. He is present in ALL; He is above ALL, through ALL, and IN ALL." (Ephesians 4:6 Mirror Study Bible)

Today I am so very proud, honored, and blessed to be Betty's husband and partner in this passionate journey to share the message of humanity's true identity. As you read her book, my hope is that you will be open minded. What do I mean by this? That you would be willing to let Spirit guide you into discovering what God believes to be true about you, even when it contradicts what you have been taught or perhaps for the first time. You have no accusers, only the perfect love of God that casts out all fear.

Thank you Betty, for all the wonderful discoveries that you have shared with me as Spirit has guided your thoughts and put words on paper. I love you.

Lloyd

Acknowledgments

I give tribute and my heartfelt gratitude to the following Brothers and Sisters, who have inspired me with their words in face to face encounters as well as from their books and YouTube presentations. I will be referencing many of them throughout the pages of my book.

Francois du Toit PhD is the author and translator of **The Mirror Study Bible** which is an ongoing labor of love. He has written several other books entitled, *Divine Embrace, God Believes in You,* and *The Logic of His Love.* His precious wife Lydia and he also co-authored a book entitled, *The Eagle Story* which has been read around the world. Allow me to share how I discovered this translation of the Bible. I will never forget the day a young man in his early 20s texted me a portion of familiar Scripture from a translation I was not familiar with. I scrolled through the words in that text and was moved in my Spirit in such a way that I needed to find out which translation he was quoting from. Here was his response. "I was searching the internet for information on our identity in Christ. I happened to come across the *Mirror Study Bible.*" Now this young man had been in our home for 2-3 years prior to this recent communication. My Hubby and I had opened our home to young men transitioning out of substance abuse and broken relationships into productive lifestyles with ongoing healing in body, mind, and soul. We often spoke to these men about knowing who they were from God's perspective. I did further research and found out more about The Mirror Word Foundation and the Author / Translator, Francois duToit. When I listened to one of his messages online in context to understanding our identity in Christ, I wept over the Scriptures like never before in my 60 + years of being a Christian. I could not wait to share with my husband, Lloyd, how Jesus revealed Himself to me as He had done with the disciples on the road to Emmaus (Luke 24:13-35) Within 24 hours of my Husband and I pondering the truth of God's unconditional love, with NO conditions added, the scales were removed from Lloyd's eyes as well. I immediately went online and ordered a copy of the Mirror Study Bible. If you are like me, you may own many translations of the Bible, but there is none to be compared with the stunning linguistic accuracy of the **words of God** within the pages of this translation. The commentary notes are invaluable for deepening your understanding of what

vi

Jesus meant when He said, *"On that day you will know that we are in seamless union with one another. I am in my father, you are in me and I am in you. (John 14:20 Mirror Study Bible)* Our identity is beautifully revealed in Jesus. God's Unconditional Love for ALL is undeniably found on every page. We joined the countless Men and Women who have found a renewed enthusiasm to read Scripture. Our souls found rest. Francois' precious helpmate / wife Lydia, has written several children's books containing the same message and passion for truth; *Little Bear and the Mirror, KAA Of the Great Kalahari,* and *King Solitaire's Big Banquet.* Both Francois and Lydia have profoundly influenced our lives. *Where Are Your Accusers?* would never have been written if it were not for my eyes being open to the Logic of God. Having heard and read the Scriptures "rightly divided", I fell in love with Jesus. I found freedom in Christ. Here is where you can find his literary works. https://app.mirrorword.net/dropins/mirror/General/homePage

William Paul Young has written several books: *The Shack, Cross Roads, Eve: A Novel, Lies We Believe about God,* and *The Pastor.* If you are one who struggled with his words, I encourage you to Google his personal testimony and come to know the rest of the story. It may help you to go beyond mere words on a page which may collide with familiar words of indoctrinations from many sources in your past. I was moved to tears as the absolute TRUTH of God's unconditional love came alive as though for the first time. I became intimately acquainted with God, Jesus, and Spirit through these life giving words of Paul Young. You can purchase his books on amazon.com and listen to him by podcast and youtube videos. I will never forget God's timing in my reading *The Shack.* This captivating book, and the "must see movie" based on the book, met a deep seeded need in my life. I needed a hug from God and I got so much more. I realized that God didn't just love me, He is "especially fond of me". There is a huge difference between these two concepts. Read the book, and you will discover the love of God in a way you may not have ever imagined. https://wmpaulyoung.com/

The Why Guy (yes, that is his pen name) has written 3 books. They are, *In Defense of God's Love, Is God Bipolar?,* and *Know Love, No Fear, No Love, Know Fear.* His no nonsense approach toward the study of the Scriptures has profoundly revolutionized my life. These books have given answers to many conundrums of doctrines I was taught to believe. He challenged me to ask the question, 'Why do I believe what I believe?' . . . and 'Why is what I believe so important to me?' The result of his research and examination of words linguistically, contextually, and culturally, struck a chord within me I could not ignore. I took the daring challenge, took the plunge into unfamiliar territory, and have never looked back. The Why Guy is the brother I never had, and I am so grateful for his encouragement in my endeavor. His precious wife, a quiet strength behind the scenes, supplied him with encouragement, support and wisdom. What a blessing for my Husband and I to have sat across the kitchen table in their home and share sweet fellowship. You can find his books on amazon.com. You will also be blessed by listening to his YouTube channel.

Don Keathley is one of the most passionate, bold, loving, and faithful teachers I have had the blessing of listening to. Though only meeting virtually, his shepherd's heart is felt undeniably. He has written, *Hell's Illusion*, and gives an incredibly clear message of God's Unconditional Love and Grace, emphasizing the Finished work of the Cross. He makes no apologies for his message which has challenged my Husband and I to look more deeply into the unquenchable LOVE and GRACE of God. He challenged us to read the Old Testament in light of Jesus. He emphasized Jesus' main Mission being to **show us the Father** through His words of absolute TRUTH. If anything in the Old Testament does not line up with Jesus' loving portrayal of His Father, in Don's own words we should "Chuck it". Those are bold words but ones we would ALL do well to implement. My Husband and I have both appreciated his consistent and faithful teaching, not growing weary in well doing. You can find his messages on YouTube entitled, "World Inclusion Network, The Digital Cathedral" You won't be disappointed.

Brad Jersak is an incredible author, speaker, and authentic lover of Jesus. He is Canadian and an orthodox pastor teacher. He has written the following books: *A More Christlike God: A More Beautiful Gospel; Her Gates Will Never Be Shut: Hell, Hope, and the New Jerusalem; A More*

Christlike Word: A More Beautiful Faith; IN: Incarnation & Inclusion, Abba & Lamb; and *The Pastor*. My husband gives testimony to the fact that the words written in Brad's book, *A More Christlike God*, impacted him the most. My favorite virtual encounter with him was his message, *The Gospel in Chairs*. His loving, deliberate, unwavering message of God's pursuit of ALL of the human race, is compelling. He has a plethora of Podcasts which will enrich your soul and leave you never doubting the unconditional Love of God. https://www.youtube.com/watch?v=N7FKhHScgUQ

C. Baxter Krueger is one of the most relaxed, laid back Theologians I have ever virtually met. His demeanor confidently invites you to enter into the Union / Unity of the Father, Son, and Spirit. His words have resonated in my mind and heart. He has written: *The Shack Revisited, The Great Dance, Patmos, Jesus, and the Undoing of Adam, God is for Us,* and *Across All Worlds.* Any feelings of hesitancy you might harbor regarding reading or listening to a Theologian will dissipate as you sense his Shepherd's heart and see his confident smile. His subtle humor will keep you coming back. https://perichoresis.org/

Dr. Caroline Leaf opened my eyes to the beautiful world of Quantum Physics. She is the author of *Switch On Your Brain, The Perfect You,* and *Think, Learn, Succeed.* She has done a brilliant work of researching the science of thought, mind and body connection as it relates to our relationship with our Creator God and to mankind. To me, her connectedness to the Scriptures, particularly the message of the apostle Paul in Romans reinforced the need for the "renewing of our minds." The Apostle Paul speaks much about this. She has interweaved the Absolute Truth of God's words with the Absolute Truth of Science. https://drleaf.com/pages/podcasts

Dr. Bruce Wauchope is one of the founding members of Perichoresis Australia. His passionate message proclaiming, "Christ is in you . . . .and you didn't put Him there", collided with my passions. His no nonsense approach to the Scriptures, not mincing words, is compelling. His humor keeps you engaged in the irrefutable truth of the Love within the "womb" of the Triune God since the beginning of time. You can look him up on the Web at https://trinityinyou.com

Malcolm Smith began teaching and preaching about the LOVE OF GOD in his early teens. He has written *The Power of the Blood Covenant*, *The Lost Secret of the New Covenant*, and many others. The message within the pages of his book, *This Son of Mine*, truly aligned with my purpose and intent in writing *Where Are Your Accusers?* The parable of the Prodigal son recorded in Luke chapter 15 is beautifully pictured in his skillful choice of words based on authenticity from research into the culture of the day. His subtitle, Discovering Your Identity in the Love of God, is a profound and beautiful message within this parable of Jesus. You can find his books on Amazon and in Barnes and Nobles BookStores. https://www.malcolmsmith.org/

CONTENT

INTRODUCTION

Have you ever asked yourself the question?

"Why do I believe what I believe?"

Why is this important? In any delivery and reception of words, communication is the goal. That may seem obvious, but rarely taken seriously. The mind and heart immediately begin to interpret words in statements and questions, forming opinions and beliefs. From the womb to the grave, words influence every facet of our life.

A diamond is referred to as a precious stone which comes from a type of igneous rock. How the diamond is cut, with many facets or "faces." holds the secret to its value and brilliance. Our identity is like a diamond. All of mankind was created to reflect, refract, and disperse the light of God's image and likeness. The extraordinary value God places on us comes from our inclusion in His unconditional love from the beginning of time.

> *We are flawless by design, not by a decision to become.*

We are flawless by design, not by a decision to become.

In the Scriptures, the origin of our identity is likened to the ancient art of masonry. Isaiah 51:1 (NIV), *"Look to the Rock from which you were cut."*

A commentary note accompanying a verse in 1 Peter 2:6 (Mirror Study Bible) says this. *"Mankind's origin and true identity is preserved and revealed again in the Rock of ages. The term "rock" in those days, represented what we call the 'hard drive' in computer language; the place where data is securely preserved for a long time. Rock fossils carry the oldest data and evidence of life."*

Though our identity is flawless, giving evidence of the life of our design, often our words are not, giving evidence of a lost identity. Deuteronomy 32:18 (NIV) "You deserted the Rock who fathered you; you forgot the God who gave you birth." When false data is entered into the computer of our mind, and misinterpreted as truth, the reflection of God's opinion is obscured. In the diamond industry this would be considered a blemish. Blemishes occur after a diamond's formation. Nothing will diminish the core value God placed on us before the foundation of the earth. But, words can and will diminish the clarity of understanding our true value and that of others. A false perception of our identity will result in a false perception of God, and vice versa.

The subtitle of this book is,
"Words matter because you matter."

Words express mindsets and beliefs which will define who we are. Their sources are based on either relative truth appealing to our 5 senses or absolute truth established by God before we were born. Relative truth is motivated by fear, performing to become. Absolute truth is motivated by love, acknowledging who I am. Words shape our identity. God's words are absolute. When man's words contradict God's words, Man's true identity is challenged.

God takes words seriously. After all, His Son, Jesus, is "the WORD." the LOGOS, the LOGIC OF GOD. (see John 1:1 and Hebrew 1:1) One would certainly conclude that His words absolutely matter because He is ABSOLUTE TRUTH.

My Husband Lloyd and I, having both been raised in Christian homes, never challenged "God's word." In fact, we were somewhat discouraged from doing so. Why?, because it was an ingrained teaching that the Bible was, is, and will always be the authoritative "Word of God." Considering the fact that there are myriads of translations of the Bible, many contradicting each other, I would ask the question, "Which Bible?" Words within Scripture were translated and interpreted for us by thousands of men and women who claimed to know and understand the Bible long before we were even born. We were never invited, let alone encouraged to think independently from what we were being taught. This is **indoctrination.**

> **"The process of teaching a person or group
> to accept a set of beliefs
> Uncritically."**
> (Oxford Languages)

"Uncritically" is a keyword, entirely relevant to my purpose and intent in writing this book. To believe anything devoid of critical thinking is to ignore logic. To ignore logic is to deny the very source of absolute truth, God's Spirit within.

> **Critical thinking is the process of applying logic
> for the sole purpose of separating truth from lies.**

In any literary work, interpretation of words must begin with a framework, if you will, of intentional and purposeful study of linguistics and context. The influences of Culture, religion, history, and even politics must be taken into consideration. When any one of these components are missing or ignored, there is a risk of misinterpretation, insertion of words, and flawed translations.

Undergirding this framework must be an unshakable brick and mortar foundation. Without this, the integrity of what we believe will be compromised. Critical thinking is the brick. Logic is the mortar. Both serve to support our development of mindsets and beliefs.

It is my observation and experience that in many cases the Scriptures have been exempt from the application of critical thinking and Logic. This has left us with a mixed message. "The Why Guy" entitled his 2nd of 4 books, "Is God Bipolar?" This proposed question certainly describes the confusion caused by man's misinterpretation of God's words. Victoria, one of my treasured granddaughters summed up this confusion in this appropriate proverbial phrase.

**"God's love is unconditional
under these conditions."**

Where Are Your Accusers? is a fulfillment of my passion to share the life changing effect of daring to ask, "Why do I believe what I believe?" By applying critical thinking and logic to words previously translated for us in Scripture, my husband and I have experienced freedom from the fears of doing so. I am not at all suggesting a mere academic approach to Scripture. Even Jesus warned against this when appealing to the Religious teachers of the law (see John 5:39). Fear has motivated many a man's interpretations of God's words.

Love cannot coexist with fear. God is Love by His very essence and being. By flawless design, we embody that Love. Words spoken or written by God or of God will always express the LOGIC of God. Our minds have the incredible responsibility to discern words of absolute truth and reject illogical words contradicting them.

In John 8:1-11, you will read the context from which I received the title for this book. Jesus was face to face with Religious Pharisees and teachers of the law, when they brought an unnamed woman before him. She was accused of committing adultery, a behavior punishable by stoning under the law. It is important to note that the Identity of all involved in this encounter was challenged in the words spoken by Jesus.

Whether an accusation is true or false, one's identity will be challenged.

Religious leader: "Teacher, this woman was caught committing adultery. Now Moses commanded us in the law that adulterers should be stoned! What would you say?"

Jesus: *He who is without sin among you, let him cast the first stone.*

Jesus: *"Where are your accusers? Has no one condemned you?"*

Woman: *"No one Lord."*

Jesus: *"Neither am I condemning you." Go and sin no more."*

Jesus' statements and questions are timeless. Every day, in some form or another, we all face words of accusation. Accusation is a strong word, rooted in expectations. Expectations come from behavioral and performance driven mindsets and beliefs. Whether an accusation is true or false, one's identity will be challenged.

This unnamed woman is a representation of you and me. The behavior and accusations made may not be the same, but the mindsets and beliefs which challenge our identity, are familiar and common to ALL. Jesus was fully aware of this woman's behavior under the law. This was not what He focused on. His concern was for this woman's perceived identity. She needed to be reminded of who Jesus knew her to be from before time began. The value Jesus placed on her was not based on her behavior but based on her birthright. The words exchanged in this short encounter between Jesus and this woman, became the foundation for the content in this book. Discovering the meaning of words, based on the exploration of linguistic study of early manuscripts, has been a life changing experience. God's words lived out in Jesus, will NEVER contradict His words, "IT IS FINISHED." The WORD/Jesus can NEVER deny who He is (2 Timothy 2:13). When the words and interpretations I was taught to believe collided with unwavering words of God's unconditional love, faith exploded in my mind and heart.

> *The value Jesus placed on her was not based on her behavior but based on her birthright.*

"The dynamic of the Gospel is the revelation of God's faith as the only valid basis for our belief . . . .God believes that righteousness reveals the life of our design. Righteousness by His faith defines life."
(see *Romans 1:17 Mirror Study Bible*)

I cannot improve upon what the writer of Hebrews so eloquently described in Hebrew 4:12 (Mirror Study Bible). This is my testimony. I have personalized this passage with no alteration to its meaning.

*"The message God spoke to **me** in Christ*
*is the most life giving and dynamic influence in **me**,*
cutting like a surgeon's scalpel, sharper than a soldier's sword,
*piercing to the deepest core of **my** conscience*
*to the dividing of **my** soul and spirit;*
ending the dominance of the sense realm
*and its neutralizing effect upon **my** spirit."*

Simply put, **"Once I was blind, but now I see."** *(John 9:23 all translations)*

My husband and I were challenged by these words spoken by Paul.

(Romans 12:2 Mirror Study Bible)
"Do not allow current religious tradition to mold you into its pattern of reasoning.
Like an inspired artist, Give attention to the detail of God's desire to find expression in YOU.
Become acquainted with Perfection.
To accommodate yourself to the delight and good pleasure of Him
Will transform your thoughts afresh from within."

For too long we have searched for perfection in performance. God desires we live in the freedom of our flawlessness.

WORDS MATTER BECAUSE YOU MATTER!

Can words on a page ever be the result of flawless motives or perfectly calculated trajectories of thought? Will my words, no matter how sincere, clever, or persuasive, ensure my intent? Reactions and responses will have been influenced by the thousands upon thousands of words encountered prior to this book's arrival. Perceptions begin to form when connections are made with words. More importantly, *words will always have an impact on our identity . . . who we perceive ourselves to be and how we perceive others.*

Further questions I asked myself were, can authors have any control over, or take responsibility for responses? Does the heart respond independent of the mind or the mind independent of the heart? It is our right, responsibility, and privilege to examine words carefully. When relative truth drives our perceptions of words, we are left with confusion and doubts. When absolute truth takes the helm of perceptions, we experience clarity and confidence. Consider these words written by C.S. Lewis, author of the well known "Chronicles of Narnia."

"The heart cannot rejoice
in what the mind rejects as false."

Can we know what absolute truth is? I believe it is more than possible. I believe it is in humanity's DNA to know, and therefore experience nothing less. Our identity originates in absolute truth.

I have chosen a curious word to describe the proverbial relationship mankind has with words throughout life; Sojourner.

Sojourner is a Hebrew term conveying the basic idea of one residing, either temporarily or permanently, in a community and place that is not their own. He or she is dependent on the "good-will" of that community for their continued existence. Words come and go . . . mostly go when you're my age. We reside, either temporarily or permanently, in a community of words that may or may not primarily be our own. *Our perception of words will determine our continued existence of wellbeing.*

Our identity originates in absolute truth.

According to Proverbs 18:21, words can either speak life, or death and most assuredly will influence our Identity. We may or may not choose our journey with words, but we do choose our destiny as it relates to our understanding and interpretation of words.

In the courtroom of our minds we have the extraordinary capability of becoming judge, juror, plaintiff or defendant. Words are powerful. They influence perceptions, followed by a trajectory of thoughts, carrying with them a calculated verdict of TRUTH or LIE. Words rarely stand alone. They become building blocks, one stacked upon another over hours, days, years or a lifetime. Words contribute to mindsets. Mindsets establish beliefs. Beliefs will dictate our attitudes and behaviors, establishing motives. Motives will always be subservient to our mindsets and can lead to justifications and rationalizations of behavior. In a court of law, determining a motive is of paramount importance in reaching a verdict and thereby understanding behavioral responses. But this is the most ambiguous step in the process. Wikipedia defines motive as: "a need that requires satisfaction." I would propose that our needs change as our perceptions of words change.

In my opinion, there are Two broad categories into which words implied or perceived will fall into;

ACCEPTANCE rooted in LOVE
or
REJECTION / rooted in FEAR.

The first and most important choice our mind has to make is to align words with Absolute Truth. This is the process of *rightly dividing*. Simply said, *separating words that envelope God's character of unconditional love from words which contradict the same.* Feeling Loved or fearful, included or separated, valued or worthless, hangs in the balance depending on that choice.

What is it that gives motivation to words, launching them like arrows in an archer's bow, destined for another's mind and heart? What is it that determines the arrow's destiny? I am proposing that IDENTITY is the motivation behind words delivered and received. "WHO AM I ?," is the heart cry of all humanity, from the womb to the grave. Our answer to this universal question gives evidence of having been significantly influenced by words. Our mindsets and beliefs regarding our perceived identity will be based on words from one of two sources; relative truth or absolute truth. Relative truth can or will result in comparisons and falsehoods about ourselves.

> *IDENTITY is the motivation behind words delivered and received.*

"Absolute Truth is something that is
true at all times and in all places.
It is something that is
always true no matter what the circumstances.
It is a fact that cannot be changed."

Logic tells me that ALL of mankind's TRUE IDENTITY is established in the ABSOLUTE TRUTH OF OUR ORIGIN.

Merriam-Webster's Dictionary defines identity as follows:

"The distinguishing character or personality of an individual formed through a process of exploring options or choices and committing to an option based upon the outcome of their explorations. Failure to establish a well-developed sense of identity can result in identity confusion."

Something, or someone, cannot be lost without first having belonged.

I agree with Webster that *"failure to establish a well developed sense of identity can result in identity confusion."* But when the premise for this establishment is relative truth based on learned behavior, we become chameleons in our character and personality; *"a person who often changes his or her beliefs or behavior in order to please others or to succeed."* (Oxford *Learner's Dictionary*). Comparing ourselves to others who have "explored their options" by comparing themselves to others who have "explored their options" is an exercise in futility and insanity.

To use some of Webster's terminology, I have established this conclusion. There is only ONE option to *"explore"* and *"commit to,"* and that is, *"Absolute Truth of ORIGIN."* Failure to establish a strong, well developed sense of Identity in this context, will inevitably result in not only confusion but also a perception of a LOST IDENTITY. The following statement may seem obvious, but often not considered. Something, or someone, cannot be lost without first having belonged.

In all reality, the answer to the question, "Who am I?" is found in the answer to a crucial question, "Whose am I?." This is my belief. The "blueprint for our identity," descriptive words used by Francois du Toit which I have embraced, goes back farther than physical conception, accompanied by generational characteristics and behavior. *The*

Absolute Truth of our ORIGIN goes back to the MIND and LOGIC of GOD. We were in His mind before the world began. You and I were made in the image and likeness of GOD. He loved us from before the beginning of time.

Dr. Caroline Leaf refers to Identity as "the perfect you." I offer you her words to consider. My conclusion is they are words of absolute truth.

"The perfect you will take you from missing the mark of being made in God's image to stepping into who you truly are. *In this way, you will move from trauma to freedom, from pain to peace, from indecision to action, from confusion to clarity, from envy to celebration, from frustration to anticipation, from being overwhelmed to being set free, from fear to courage, from suppressing issues to having the courage to face them, from numbing thoughts to capturing them, from passivity to passion, and from hopelessness to hope." [Dr. Caroline Leaf pg. 35 "The Perfect You." See acknowledgements]*

Your understanding of who you are because of who you belong to is essential. Most of what we believe is what we were taught to believe, often with no choice. Why we believe what we believe becomes our responsibility and ultimately our choice. Sad to say, most of us were never encouraged to think for ourselves. In some cases we were discouraged from and shunned if we dared to challenge what we were taught to believe, especially if those beliefs were founded on religious doctrines.

The Apostle Paul speaks often about the "RENEWING of the MIND." The mind can become our adversary, or our valued ally by our choice. In Genesis 3, Adam experienced the former. In Matthew 4, Jesus is our example of the latter. We should never underestimate or discount the power of words over our mind and heart. **Never stop asking why you believe what you believe**. If what you believe envelops the absolute truth of God's character of unconditional love, God's words will stand the test of scrutiny and Spirit will confirm. Your heart will rejoice in the truth. If what you believe contradicts God's character, Spirit will lovingly guide you into ALL TRUTH. God will continue to speak words of unconditional love throughout all eternity.

WHAT IS ABSOLUTE TRUTH?
JESUS ANSWERS,
"I AM"
therefore
"YOU ARE."

TRUTH OR INSANITY
IT'S YOUR CHOICE

I begin this chapter by referencing an old Hymn written by Frederick M. Lehman entitled, *"The Love of God."* The story behind the lyrics of the 3rd verse is profound. It brings a relevance and depth of meaning congruent with my focus within this chapter.

"Sometime around 1917, Lehman, preparing to relocate to California, was at a camp meeting in a Midwestern State and heard an evangelist end his message by quoting what became the third stanza of Lehman's song "The Love of God." The preacher said that these lines had been found penciled on the wall of a patient's room in an insane asylum, after he had been carried to his grave. The assumption was that this inmate had scratched out the words in moments of sanity."

"Could we with ink the ocean fill,
and were the skies of parchment made,
were every stalk on earth a quill,
and every man a scribe by trade;
To write the Love of God above

> *would drain the ocean dry;*
> *Nor could the scroll contain the whole,*
> *though stretched from sky to sky."*

What drove this man to insanity and subsequently into an asylum/prison is not recorded. One can only surmise what caused a breakthrough in his mind and heart to inscribe such words. I believe supposition in this case is based on truth and worthy of our consideration.

David Cuschieri, a well known author, writes this statement.

> *"The mind is a powerful force.*
> *It can enslave us or empower us.*
> *It can plunge us into the depths of misery*
> *or take us to the heights of ecstasy."*

Behind prison walls, this man was faced with an unseen battle in his mind. There was a voice of logic, Spirit within, speaking God's words of Acceptance and Love. These words collided with words of condemnation and fear. He was confronted with a choice to be made. The words etched on that wall gave evidence of his choosing life giving words over words of death and destruction. Words of relentless Unconditional Love brought his mind and heart into alignment with God's words of Absolute Truth. He rejoiced in what his mind recognized as truth. His true identity was validated.

Most of us are familiar with the definition of insanity as, "doing the same thing over and over again and expecting different results." Why do we equate insanity with behavior? Perhaps it is because behavior is tangible and relative to our deliberate choices. The following words are given as synonyms for the word insanity: Illogical, Foolish, Senseless, Irrational

Words opposite of insanity: truth, of sound mind, certainty, balance
(Roget's 21st Century Thesaurus, Third Edition Copyright c 2013 by Lief Group)

I am not disputing the fact that there can be uncontrollable, physiological causes for mental illness. Those who have a loved one with Alzheimer's or Dementia have witnessed the heartache of cognitive and behavioral insanity. But oh the anguish, to witness a loved one who fell prey to words of rejection, condemnation, and judgment, driving them to believe lies about themselves, leading to death by suicide. This is a travesty.

Words will always be received in conjunction with perceptions.

We have all experienced moments of temporary insanity as a result of mindsets and beliefs beholding to generational rhetoric. But, there is one fundamental question needing to be answered when faced with contradiction in the heart and mind. A.W. Tozer, a revered Pastor, Teacher, and Author, is renowned for his many thought provoking quotes. My Husband Lloyd, reminded me of one which stirred his heart many years ago, and he has never forgotten it.

> *"What comes into our minds when we think about God is the most important thing about us."*

Lloyd, beloved and revered by me, added this provocative thought.

> ***"The most important thing about us is WHAT WE BELIEVE GOD BELIEVES TO BE TRUE ABOUT US."***

Words rarely stand alone when arriving at their destinations of mind and heart. They collide with established beliefs. It is so important to understand that what we believe is nothing more than an acceptance of and agreement with words. Words will always be received in conjunction with perceptions. Applying logic and thereby rightly dividing words of truth from lies, will indicate either a sound mind based on absolutes or one given to misinterpretation based on lies. In either choice, the mind will "reside" with these words "temporarily" or "permanently" forming a mindset and belief.

According to Roger Smalling D.Min:

> **"Logic is an absolute . . .**
> *for existence cannot BE what it is,*
> *and NOT BE what it is.*
> *It is obvious therefore that*
> *TRUTH and LOGIC are inseparable."*

He goes on to explain Logic vs. Reason.

"The difference between logic and reason is the same as between mathematics and a mathematician. A simple arithmetic formula, such as 4X4=16, is a mathematical fact, regardless of how many third-graders get it wrong in learning their multiplication tables. The logic of the arithmetic corresponds to the real world. If four rabbits multiply four times, we have sixteen rabbits regardless of whether anyone in the forest knows about it. Math makes no mistakes. Mathematicians do."

In my research the difference between logic and reason supports the importance of absolute truth. If we look at logic being inseparable from Truth, and reason being the power of the mind to think, understand and form judgments logically, we have to rightly divide words. This necessitates a standard of absolutes in order to avoid illogical conclusions and confusion. Wikipedia defines Logical Truth and Absolute Truth as *"one of the most fundamental concepts in logic. In other words, a logical truth is a statement which is not only true, but one which is true under all interpretations of its logical components."*

Words without the embodiment of facts, validity, reality, and logic, will result in a plethora of relative truths. This would include variations in interpretation. Manipulation of thoughts and emotions with relativity, can result in inconsistencies at best, and lies at worst. A fact, by its very definition, cannot be logically disputed nor changed by reason. Words based on facts become validated and therefore become a *Therefore, TRUTH and LOGIC are inseparable."* reality, not based on emotions but on logic. We don't make up facts. Facts are accepted as concrete realities.

I must make a bold statement at this point. In my opinion there is one book which has somehow escaped the scrutiny of logic. That is the Bible. I will develop this further in Chapter 5.5. God's words are absolute truth. Man's words, unless interpreted with the logic of God, cannot be considered absolute truth, and will end in confusion and broken relationships.

Google Search gave me these stats. As of Sept. 2020 the full Bible has been translated into 704 languages. The New Testament itself has been translated into an additional 1,551 languages, and Bible portions or stories into 1,160 languages. I found this statement, regarding original texts of Scripture, by James Oppenheimer-Crawford:

"While it is true that we do not have the actual autographs, the original texts, our studies have gotten to the point, by comparison and educated studies of a large number of different sources, that we are for the vast majority, very confident of the meaning of the text. It is true that in some cases, our opinions of what the texts actually mean will vary, depending on our individual theologies. After all, if you are pretty sure how things are, and the Bible doesn't slightly jibe with that, you would be tempted to rationalize a slight difference in translation to bring the Bible translation into agreement with what you already know is so. These cases are, as you can imagine, not trivial, but at the same time, for the most part, this kind of disagreement is the exception. So you are wise to choose a version which your denomination approves."

I have to disagree with his premise and conclusive statements. At the time of my writing this book, there are more than 45,000 denominations globally. A common definition of the word denomination is a particular religious group which has slightly different beliefs from other groups within the same faith. If the Scripture is the authoritative word of God . . . and if Logic and truth are inseparable . . . why so many translations and denominations? Consider these words:

"Scriptures have been used to justify some of the greatest atrocities in human history. People were tortured, burned at the stake and multitudes murdered, based on somebody's understanding of the Scriptures. Jesus, Paul, and believers throughout the ages, face their greatest opposition from those who knew the Scriptures."
(quoted from The incarnation-Code pg. 24 The Acts of the Apostles Volume 1 ISBN 978-1-7764104-0-8 copyright 2012 by Francois du Toit)

I have to agree with His analysis. It is a travesty but true. We may not have any of the original manuscripts of the Bible, but we do have the Spirit of God within us who desires to lead us into all truth. One of the phrases Jesus uses over and over again in Scripture is, **"I tell you the truth."** In chapter one, I made a statement that identity is the motivation behind words. *Mankind's identity is an example of Absolute, logical Truth.* If our identity is embodied in the absolute truth of our origin, we'd best interpret God's words in this context.

Before Jesus was crucified, the exchange of words between Jesus and Pilate are worthy of paramount consideration. *(see John 18:30-19:22 Mirror Study Bible)* A Roman Governor named Pontius Pilate, asked Jesus, "What is truth?" There was a battle going on in the mind of Pilate. The charges brought against Jesus were behaviorally driven. In the words of the Jewish authorities, he was "an evil doer." Here is the immediate context to this question.

Pilate asked Jesus, "Are you the King of the Jews?"

Jesus responded, "My Kingdom has nothing in common with the political or religious systems of this world; it does not originate out of their structures." Pilate then said, "So you are a king?"

Jesus replied, "You say that I am a King. My destiny was to be born in the flesh and for this purpose have I come into the world to bear testimony to the truth. Everyone who recognizes their true origin, hears my voice."

Indoctrinated beliefs collided with ABSOLUTE TRUTH.

Pilate then asked Him, **"What is truth?"**

Pilate did not wait for an answer to his question. He was face to face with TRUTH, but was blind and would not see, deaf and would not hear. He did not recognize who Jesus was. In this he displayed the fact that he was operating out of a lost identity.

In 2015 my Husband's and my indoctrinated beliefs collided with absolute truth, creating a paradigm shift in our minds and hearts. Reading and listening to Jesus' words where logic was applied, became "Living and powerful."

(Hebrews 4:12 in the Mirror Study Bible)

"The message God spoke to us in Christ, is the most life giving and dynamic influence in us, cutting like a surgeon's scalpel, sharper than a soldier's sword, piercing to the deepest core of human conscience, to the dividing of soul and spirit; ending the dominance of the sense realm and neutralizing effect upon the human spirit. In this way a person's spirit is freed to become the ruling influence again in the thoughts and intentions of their hearts. The scrutiny of this living Sword-Logos detects every possible disease, discerning the body's deepest secrets where joint and bone-marrow meet."

Hebrews 4:12 is not describing the power of a book.
It is a description of the power of THE WORD . . . JESUS.

Understanding this is the first step to understanding that Christ in ALL is the indwelling logos (Word) of God. His Spirit validates our identity.

"The truth about mankind's authentic sonship, and the image and likeness of the invisible Father of the human race, is evidenced in me and confirmed in my work of redeeming the human race from the futile ways they inherited from their fathers." (John 18:37 Mirror Study Bible)

The misinterpretation of God's words continues to this day. The ongoing empty rhetoric and lies of God's condemnation, judgment and separation are ever present in our religious instruction throughout history around the world. Much of this teaching can be traced back to man endorsing words of Old Testament writers who had an incomplete picture of who God was. Jesus had not yet come to display the Father. Many of their words were a perception based on outside religious and political influences. Translators of manuscripts were also influenced by surrounding nations and cultures. This included similar beliefs in many fictitious gods and alleged demonic beings. Extra biblical accounts reveal periods of violent political and religious upheavals leading to power and control over what people were taught to believe. Fear was portrayed in the words spoken by Old Testament writers, and Fear was incorporated in the translations from later manuscripts. Between the Old and New Testaments, there is a recorded 400 year period of time when God was believed to have remained "silent." Perceived silence does not refute God's indwelling the lives of all mankind. Nor does it validate a belief that mankind was separated from the love of God or rejected by God. That would be illogical based on the fact that He/Christ dwells in us from birth.

Please consider looking up "The Gospel in Chairs," "A Beautiful Gospel," presented by Brad Jersak. You can find it on YouTube. God's loving pursuit of ALL mankind to experience an inseparable love relationship with them, is clearly portrayed throughout the pages of Scripture. This will only be recognized in light of God's character of unconditional love and awakening to our true identity. *Our knowing the truth of what God believes to be true about us, is foundational to our Spiritual, mental and physical well being.* But wonder if we do not?

(Romans 3:3&4 Mirror Study Bible)

"The question is, how does someone's failure to believe God affect what God believes? Can their unbelief cancel God's faith? God's word is not under threat! In fact if all of mankind fails, Truth remains intact. Truth is defined in God; It is neither challenged nor vindicated by human experience. Contradiction does not intimidate or diminish the faith of God. Scripture records that God stands justified in his own word; it confirms that God's promise and purpose are not compromised through mankind's failure; neither is God's reputation threatened by our behavior."

If all of mankind fails, Truth remains intact.

There is such freedom in choosing to believe and embrace God's words of absolute truth. I will close with these words of Jesus.

"To take my word to its complete conclusion, and then to abide in seamless union with its logic, is to truly be my disciples. In this abiding you will fully know the truth about who you are, and this knowing will be your freedom."

(John 8:31-32 Mirror Study Bible)

CHAPTER 3

TRUE LOVE
FROM THE BEGINNING

As I write this, the 2021 Summer Olympics are taking place. When the athletes enter into their events, there is a sense of total equality with their competitors in qualification and potential. Placement results in the past competitions do not define them in this moment. On this day, at this time, there is a new confidence accompanied by hopes and dreams.

But I see a very threatening trajectory of thought that can loom over new beginnings . . . fear of failure. Behaviorally driven hopes and dreams can sabotage not only one's confidence, but more importantly, undermine one's identity. One world champion athlete was quoted as saying, "I feel the weight of the world on my shoulders." *When our identity is defined by our performance, we sacrifice knowing who we are on the altar of striving to become.* Knowing our beginning, our place of origin, is to awaken to our identity. No matter the challenge we will be able to say as David in the Psalms; *"nothing will shake my well being" (Psalm 16 and 62 any translation)*

Our physical life is not our beginning. Just as Jesus' life did not begin in a manger, our lives did not begin in a hospital delivery room, taxi cab or family car, birthing center or home. Life did not even begin in our parents' minds. We were in God's mind from the beginning. *We were God's will long before any will, or ill will of man.* God is the author of life. We were divinely conceived in love. Our beginning is in the embrace of God's love. We were created to be loved, and to love others in the same way. This love is unconditional with no expectations or conditions to receive that love. Our life is a declaration of perfection and innocence from the beginning and throughout all eternity. God's opinion is not dependent on our behavior. God's opinion is based on who He is and who He says we are.

WHAT WE BELIEVE GOD BELIEVES TO BE TRUE ABOUT US
is essential for our well being.

Feelings of Guilt and shame, relative to our earthly beginnings, are based on perceptions derived from words of man and not from God. We were made in His image and likeness. Our value and worth is not determined by our behavior or external characteristics.

(1 Samuel 16:7b NIV)
The Lord does not look at the things people look at.
People look at the outward appearance,
But the Lord looks at the heart."

I pray these words will bring comfort to those who were labled, "oops" babies, or those born as a result of rape or incest. You were not a mistake. No matter under what circumstances you were conceived, nor what you look like, no matter what you have said or done in your lifetime, no matter what words were spoken, or neglected to be said to you when desperately needed, ***YOU ARE LOVED UNCONDITIONALLY!*** Your beginning started in the mind, will, and heart of God, and this is absolute truth! I also want to say, I believe with all of my being that every heartbeat silenced by the will of man or woman is beating today. It is a precious life embraced in Jesus' loving arms, a gift from God.

> *We were God's will long before any will, or ill will of man.*

I can also declare that Jesus' arms of love, grace, and mercy, extend to and embrace ALL those who participated in such decisions made, and procedures performed, to silence that heartbeat.

From conception on, we are defined by behavior. When a baby is in the womb, they can be viewed as an inconvenience or annoyance. After birth their behavior is on display. Personalities and temperaments begin to develop. Descriptions are based on whether they sleep through the night, or how often they cry. We may look at that sweet little mop haired or bald headed baby with love and delight as they are sleeping soundly and quietly in their crib. But, that opinion can quickly change at two o'clock in the morning when awakened from much needed sleep. Behavior will always evoke responses and reactions. If we do not focus on one's declared innocence with love, we will begin to fall into a trap of defining people based on behavior and our expectations to perform.

A couple of years ago I was reading William Paul Young's book, *Lies we believe about God*. The first chapter is entitled, "God Loves us, but doesn't like us." This resonates with me. I truly believe most folk will not take issue with the statement, "God loves me." How could we? After all, "Jesus loves me, this I know, for the bible tells me so." Right? But to be "liked" by God is to have his approval. To be "disliked" by God means He is disappointed in me. When we believe it is our "good" or "bad" behavior which qualifies or disqualifies us to receive approval from God, our perception of God's love becomes a lie. I have seen this time and time again, not only in my own family, but in the lives of those behind prison walls.

There are three words indelibly etched in my mind from childhood that shaped my understanding and perception of God. When these words were spoken in succession, within the context of scripture, they carried much weight.

disappointment,

rejection,

and

consequences,

I associated consequences as coming from God, because of my "disobedience." These consequences would range from His disappointment in me to outright rejection of me, either temporarily or for all eternity. To avoid eternal separation from God, I had to "pray the sinner's prayer" and "ask Jesus into my heart." This made me his child for all eternity. This one time prayer would guarantee my never being rejected and separated from God after I died. With that being said, there are some religions which teach that eternal security is still in question depending on certain unpardonable offenses. It does seem to be a universal belief that a child of God still needs to "confess sin" daily to remove all reasonable doubt of His disapproval and separation. I am convinced that these beliefs are based on the doctrines of men which adhere to the teaching that

- God cannot look upon sin.
- Sin separates me from God.

Another misconception I had formed in my mind was this. Consequences were always due to poor behavioral choices resulting in negative effects. In this context, the familiar phrase, "suffer the consequences" is very appropriate, and is usually associated with punishment. But by definition, the word consequence does not simply imply good or bad results from good or bad actions. When looking at its meaning, I was also surprised to find that *a consequence is not limited to a result of a particular behavior, but could also be the result of conditions.* Webster's Dictionary definition is as follows:

"A conclusion derived through logic: inference, something produced by a cause or necessarily following from a set of conditions. The word consequence infers value, seriousness, noteworthiness, and essentiality."

In this context I would have to conclude that a belief formed from a mindset becomes a condition, and the behavior that follows becomes the effect and consequence. To me, when the Apostle Paul spoke of "the laws of the harvest," he was describing consequences . If we plant corn we will harvest corn. If we jump from the top floor of the Empire State building, gravity will remain in effect and we will hit the pavement.

Consequences are not from God. They are the results of mindsets, choices, and behaviors. When we realize that these effects are valuable and essential for our growth, we can examine them logically. We will then have an opportunity to embrace God's logic in the process. He sees our consequences as an opportunity to always bring us back to the truth of our origin, being in a "womb" of unconditional LOVE from the beginning. When applying this truth to the consequences of our lives, we are given a fresh opportunity to experience God's never ending involvement in our choices, affirming His unconditional love. He often will not intervene to alter the course of the consequence. In these cases, our mindset and belief must be; GOD IS GOOD and GOD IS LOVE in His essence. This is the absolute truth. I made a statement earlier in this chapter which I want to emphasize here.

Consequences are not from God. They are the results of mindsets, choices, and behaviors.

We were created to be unconditionally loved, and to love in that same way. How many times have you been disappointed in someone else, be it a loved one or a complete stranger? We form our own standards for behavior. We declare a verdict before gathering the truth. *We sacrifice compassion and empathy on the altar of our conditions and expectations.* This destroys relationships and does not send a message of God's unconditional love.

If you think about it, disappointment can only come when conditions or expectations are not met. Therefore, *God will NEVER be disappointed in you.* We would do well to adopt the same mindset toward others. The Apostle Paul truly experienced and grasped the unconditional love of God. Consider these words in 2 Corinthians 5:15,16 *(Mirror Study Bible)*

"If all were included in his death, they were equally included in His resurrection. This unveiling of His love redefines human life! Whatever reference we could have of ourselves outside of our association with Christ, is no longer relevant. Therefore, from now on, I no longer know anyone according to the flesh! I no longer see people from a human point of view. **By considering Christ from God's point of view, we discover ourselves and every other human life from God's point of view!"**

God will NEVER be disappointed in you.

As I pondered these words, my thoughts were challenged by these questions. Doesn't God have the right to have conditions and expectations of his creation? Isn't God in control? The following two descriptions of God helped me to put such thoughts in perspective.

"Everything that is begins in Him; whether in the heavenly realm or upon the earth, visible or invisible, He is the original blueprint of every order of justice and every level of authority, be it kingdoms or governments, principalities jurisdictions; the original form of all things were founded by Him and created for him."
(Colossians 1:16 Mirror Study Bible)

Now let's take a look at how His character was displayed in Jesus, remembering that He is God in flesh. Phipippians 2:7 is a beautiful description of control encapsulated in Humility. *(Mirror Study Bible)*

"His (Jesus') mission however, was not to prove His Deity,
but to embrace our mankind.
Emptied of His reputation as God,
He fully embraced our physical human form;
born in our resemblance
He identified Himself as the servant of the human race."

What a dichotomy of thought! God of all creation, who holds the Universe together, every galaxy in place, chose to experience every physical, emotional, and spiritual consequence common to mankind. He identified Himself in our humanity, that we might identify ourselves in His deity. Consider the following as food for thought:

- Jesus was born in a manger . . . not a palace.
- Jesus had his angels give His birth announcements to shepherds, not Kings.
- Jesus rode into Jerusalem on a donkey, not on a white horse.
- Jesus chose fishermen, a tax collector, a treasurer, and political zealots as His students, not the well educated.
- He did not defend Himself when He stood before Pilate.
- He was silent as the Jews shouted, "Give us Barabbas!" (a convicted criminal) and "CRUCIFY HIM!" Jesus, an innocent man.
- He died at the hands of angry men and lovingly cried out, "Father, Forgive them, for they know not what they do."

God will always relinquish Control
to gain a relationship with YOU!

I can say with confidence that from the beginning of time *God's purpose is NOT TO CONTROL YOU, but to LOVE YOU.*

Does God care about our choices and behavior? He deeply cares. But He will always enter into the consequences of our choices with love, grace and mercy while whispering, "I love you and I am not disappointed in you." When we choose to ignore Him, He will never separate from us or withhold His love. Concern for His reputation is never a factor. Sad to say, this is often a motive behind parental discipline and control over "bad" behavior. He will never view us or treat us as a failure, loser, or mistake. Have you ever dared to believe in this kind of Love? Every breath is taking us to a new beginning of our choosing. When confronted with consequences, our minds are faced with a choice to walk in the awareness of His unconditional Love, or in fear, embracing a perception of disappointment, judgment, and separation from God.

Please read the following scripture carefully. I am going to personalize it by inserting "you" and "your" in place of "our" and "we."

"He (Jesus) rescued the integrity of your original design and revealed that YOU have always been His own from the beginning, even before time was. This has nothing to do with anything you did to qualify or disqualify yourself. We are not talking about religious good works or karma here. Jesus unveils grace to be the eternal intent of God! Grace celebrates your precreation innocence and now declares your redeemed union with God in Christ Jesus."
(2 Timothy 1:9 Mirror Study Bible)

> *God's purpose is NOT TO CONTROL YOU, but to LOVE YOU.*

When we embrace God's thoughts about us from the beginning, we are returning to our first Love whether we believe it or not. When we Rightly divide God's Words of unconditional love, from Man's words of conditional love, we find the truth of our origin. We find our true identity . . .

We find TRUE LOVE.

WHO OR WHAT IS THE ADVERSARY?

Recorded in Genesis 1:26-28 God is about to create man in "His image according to His likeness". These were God's words, but what do they mean? He certainly is not referring to physical characteristics for there are no two fingerprints alike. Furthermore it makes no sense to believe we are "born sinners" when said to be made in the image and likeness of a perfectly sinless God. Image simply means a visual representation. So what does that image look like? If Jesus is the physical expression of God's unconditional love, then dare we say the same of ourselves?

When God said, "Let US make man in OUR image", unconditional Love was already in effect. When God created us, we were ushered into an unprecedented love relationship between the Father, son, and Spirit. From the beginning this was God's purpose and intent in the creation of mankind. There were no expectations or conditions. Our inclusion was not by invitation but by design. In other words, we did not put ourselves there by choice. This relationship was defined even before we were in our mother's womb. **Who and whose we are was established long before we ever made a choice to believe it.** Being made in His image and likeness not only gives us a position within this love relationship, we are also given a purpose to know ourselves as Jesus saw himself. In other words to "have the mind of Christ." In Philippians 2:5 Paul wrote these words.

"Let this mind be in you which was also in Christ Jesus" (NKJV)

"The way Jesus saw himself is the only valid way to see yourself!"
(Mirror Study Bible)

I feel it's important to look into this a little further. Most, if not all religions emphasize God being in control. This context strongly suggests the opposite. This passage of Scripture can be summed up in one word . . . HUMILITY. Jesus was not a puppet on a string manipulated by God, nor are we robotic creatures under Jesus' control. Puppets and robots will never experience a relationship of love. Control infers Hierarchy, and there is no hierarchy in the relationship between God the Father, God the Son and God the Spirit. They are in complete harmony with one another within the circle of perfect Love. Why is this important? Control and Pride are in the root system of the tree of the knowledge of Good and evil spoken of in the Genesis story.

We are born with the mind of Christ. Being like-minded, involves a conscious choice to believe God's words and to bring our thoughts into alignment with them. When faced with thoughts contradictory to God's, a choice will have to be made in our mind. The choice will always be rooted in truth or a lie, love or fear, humility or pride. It will be made on the basis of an awareness of His love being unconditional or a false perception of having to earn His love based on my good behavior. When we embrace the intrinsic value and worth God placed on us, exempt from any so-called good or bad behavior, we will cease striving to become and rest in the absolute truth of our **like minded identity**. In the mind of God, I am enough, I am loved.

Choices, when activated, will have stunning consequential effects. Choices will rarely stand alone. They build one upon another. Words then become catalysts in choices. God's words are no exception. I will say this most assuredly. *God's words will never contradict His character of Love and therefore will never be adversarial.* He will never change his mind about words spoken from eternity past, present or future for they are absolute. Remember, "Absolute Truth is something that is true at all times and in all places. It is something that is always true no matter what the circumstances. It is a fact that cannot be changed."

> *God's words will never contradict His character of Love and therefore will never be adversarial.*

This is good news because this means *God will never change His mind about us.* Every choice we make will be within the parameters of God's will. Man's choice will never negate what is. We must stop looking at the account in Genesis with a focus on a command given by a controlling God to a man expected to obey with impending judgment and wrath to suffer if he disobeyed. (AKA make the wrong choice in "trees"). It was never a choice between obeying God and thereby earning His love and acceptance, or disobeying God and experiencing denial of love with rejection. This would be a controlling, law focused, works oriented, reward driven love relationship which is no relationship at all. This emphasis undermines the very purpose and intent of God for us to know who we are as we have always been known by God.

Consider Jesus' words given to a controlling, law driven group of religious leaders recorded in John 5:38-42. (Mirror Study Bible) Today God's desire for mankind to know who He is, and who He declares us to be, has not changed.

"Your doubting Him whom the Father has sent, shows that you have not taken His word to its full conclusion. You scrutinize the Scriptures tirelessly, assuming that in them you embrace the life of the ages-Yet I am what the Scriptures are all

about. Still you refuse to resort to me as the very source of the life you seek. I am not anchoring my belief in people's opinion but what I observe about you, is that God's love does not resonate within you! You're so obsessed with the rule book that all you see is a god of wrath and miss out on God's love!"

What a powerful statement. Now let's look at the imagery given in Genesis chapter 2 of two specific trees in the garden. I do not believe, even for a second, that God created a landscape with two trees to tempt or manipulate Adam into a particular choice. What's more, God did not have a premeditated plan of punishment for a choice made contrary to His desire. Symbolically the fruit from the "Tree of Life" encompassed all manner of undeniable, conclusive and absolute truth of who God is . . . Love, and who Adam was . . . God's own beloved son. To "eat" from this tree would result in the certainty and truth of Adam's original design. His declared innocence and established identity was manifested in the sweet fruit of God's Spirit.

> ***"To Love is to Know God.***
> ***To know God is to love."***
> *(1 John 4:7 Mirror Study Bible)*

In contrast, the fruit from the "Tree of the knowledge of good and evil" symbolized all manner of ambiguous rhetoric, lies and deception about God and man. To "eat" from its branches, resulted in doubt, confusion, and debate with regard to the truth, manifesting in a Lost identity and sin consciousness. Focusing on behavior is sin consciousness. Do not confuse this with being conscious of sin. When equating sin with behavior it takes us down a slippery slope, out of the realm of truth and into the trap of deception. It would be like treating symptoms without having a proper diagnosis. *Sin consciousness was never to be our place of residence.* I will develop this further in the last chapter of this book.

"Your spirit effortlessly bears the rich harvest of love, joy, peace, patience, kindness, goodness, integrity, gentleness and self control; all these individually

reveal the irresistible attraction of the inner-life of our design. (They are not fading, fragile emotions produced by willpower. This is the fruit of what you know in your spirit to be true about you. Fruit is the effortless spontaneous expression of the character of the tree. Rest in the awareness and assurance of who you really are!) Legalism can neither match or contradict this. There is no law against love! (Love does not compete with law; love is extravagant in its exhibition of the Christ life.)" (Galatians 5:22 & 23 Mirror Study Bible)

Going back to chapter 3 of Genesis, Adam was faced with a choice which would impact him and symbolically all mankind forever. There were 2 questions asked of Adam within the context of this choice. Let's take a look at these questions in an abbreviated form. In this case my intent is not to ignore context but rather to place emphasis on who is asking the question.

1. "Did God actually say . . . ?"
2. "Who told you . . . ?"

It is important to me that you understand my logic in determining the source of the first question. It is my belief that this question originated in Adam's mind and not from a being disguised as a snake, called Satan, with a capital "S." Simply stated, *satan means adversary or accuser.* When this word was penned in the early manuscripts, it was not capitalized. This would suggest that *the adversarial words entertained by Adam were not coming from a distinct being outside of Adam, but rather from within Adam's own mind.*

Sin consciousness was never to be our place of residence.

This was a game changer for me. All my life I was taught that Adam had a conversation with the devil in the form of a snake. Often today within religion we have defaulted to a belief in entities outside of ourselves, to explain and even excuse our choices. "The devil made me do it!", combined with a mindset of guilt, shame and fear, can lead to mental anguish and illness and at times even a search for some form of exorcism. Furthermore I would suggest that we have been influenced to believe words to be true simply because they are written in our Bibles or the Scriptures. These two words, in and of themselves, can subliminally hold power over us, as implied in Jesus' words mentioned earlier in this chapter. "You search the scriptures tirelessly assuming that in them you embrace the life of the ages . . . ." Here are my observations with regard to these two questions.

Adversarial words will always undermine the ABSOLUTE TRUTH of our original design.

The first question originated in Adam's mind, challenging God's words. The second question came from the mind of God, challenging Adams perception of himself, and ultimately Adams perception of God.

The first question came before a choice was made by Adam.
The second question came after Adam's choice was made.

The first question was rooted in Adam doubting God's words.
The second question was grounded in God's words of certainty.

The first question intimated God's words were not enough and Adam was incomplete. He had to do something to become.
The second question affirmed the truth of Adam's innocence and completeness in God's Love void of any expectations in behavior.

Adversarial words will always undermine the ABSOLUTE TRUTH of our original design. We can't prevent birds of prey from landing on our heads, but we can prevent them from building a nest. When "words of prey" in any form and from any source come into our mind and are allowed to linger and "build a nest," our trajectory of thought will be influenced and potentially altered leaving an entanglement of twigs and twine.

(*2 Timothy 1:7* Mirror Study Bible)
"Become fully acquainted with His gift in you, There is nothing timid about it;
the dynamic of a mind liberated in the spirit of love
a mind saved from tolerating inferior thoughts
is fearless and unstoppable."

Being vigilant and discerning in our sojourney with words and choosing to be like minded with the Logic of God, will result in fearlessness, courage, and boldness. This is to understand and embrace our true identity.

"IT IS FINISHED"

Every day we are constantly harvesting words and are left with a yield. Even when left to ourselves, we are harvesting self talk. So let's look at the old school practice of harvesting wheat, which even with modern machinery, follows the same principles. When harvesting wheat, threshing and winnowing are needed to obtain the pure grain. Threshing involves beating the wheat to loosen it from the chaff which encases the wheat. Winnowing is when the wheat is thrown into the air for the wind to blow away the chaff. What is left is the pure grain.

Words contain "wheat" and "chaff". We must "beat" words to loosen chaff (LIES) from the wheat (TRUTH). I would liken this process to critical thinking. Applying logic to words is crucial. This starts with challenging our beliefs by asking, Why do I believe them? Source and context are of utmost importance. Chaff mixed with wheat compromises the value of the harvest, not the value of the land. Words of truth mixed with words of lies result in a harvest of beliefs and behaviors which do not reflect the value God places on us. In both analogies the abundant life giving harvest was forfeited.

"*What was "It" that Jesus finished, when was "it" finished, and for whom?*"

Our minds are constantly faced with harvesting, threshing and winnowing words. Our hearts are crying out for TRUTH . . . pure "wheat". It is our responsibility to apply the LOGIC of God (*Threshing*) to that harvest of words. We then must courageously throw the loosened words of "wheat" and "chaff" up into the wind of Spirit (*Winnowing*). When trusting the Spirit to blow away the chaff, exposing the lies, our minds and hearts will rejoice in a rich harvest.

Moving forward, I wish to examine three familiar words known in the majority of Biblical teachings. I write them today with purpose and intent, as though "hearing" them for the first time. They have not only captured my attention, but radically impacted my perception, understanding, and interpretation of God's words within Scripture. Embracing these words has yielded a rich harvest.

"It is finished"
(John 19:30 any translation)

These are the last three words Jesus spoke while suspended on a cross. They were foundational in my Christian upbringing. Christianity speaks often of "the finished work of Christ". The indoctrination of biblical interpretations over my 65+ years ran deep within. My beliefs were unwavering, as one who was passionate to know the truth. I knew what I was taught, and adopted the theological terminology and the doctrines supporting my beliefs.

As I was writing this chapter, and applying logic to Scripture, I came to an impasse in my mind and heart. My passion to know the truth and have His mind and acknowledge His unconditional love, has never died. I dared to ask myself, "*What was "It" that Jesus finished, when was "it" finished, and for whom?*" His death, burriel, resurrection and ascension are the culmination

40

to His incarnation, all beautifully expressed in Jesus' final words. By applying logic to the overall context, I began to question what I was taught to believe. Consider this grammar lesson on the word "finished" as recorded in the commentary note below and validated in my own research.

*"The word **tetelestai** (finished) communicates the final consummation of all things; –**everything is now concluded!**– John records this powerful word in the Perfect Passive Tense, which denotes an action which is COMPLETED IN THE PAST, but THE EFFECTS of which are regarded as CONTINUING INTO THE PRESENT WITHOUT END."*
(commentary note on John 19:30 by Francois DuToit)

This example of the scriptures being rightly divided, has led to my conclusive statement below.

**The message and effect of the cross
is not confined to a single,
well documented event in history.
Rather, the message and effect is timeless.**

With that being said, let's look at Jesus' words spoken prior to the events on the cross.

*"In that day you will know
that we are in seamless union
with one another!*
**I am in my Father, you are in me and
I am in you!"**
(John 14:20 Mirror Study Bible)

What did these words mean in the context of the past, present and continuing finished work of the Cross? I asked God to reveal the truth to me. Tears literally filled my eyes as Spirit led me to John 17:26 and Hebrews 1:3 respectively *(Mirror Study Bible)*. The first passage is John's record of Jesus' prayer in the Garden of Gethsemane prior to His arrest and subsequent death. The Hebrew's passage compliments Jesus' prayer by emphasizing the completed work of Christ.

> *"I have made the essence of your being Known to them*
> *so that they may know you by name;*
> *And I will also give them understanding to know*
> *that the same love wherewith you have loved me*
> *is in them, even as I am in them!"*

> *"Jesus is the crescendo of God's conversation with humankind;*
> *He gives context and content to the authentic thought.*
> *Everything that God had in mind for mankind is voiced in Him.*
> *Jesus is God's language. His name declared His mission.*
> *As SAVIOR OF THE WORLD he truly REDEEMED*
> *the image and likeness of the invisible God*
> *and made him apparent again in human form as in a mirror."*

That's the "IT"

REDEMPTION is a declaration of that which has already been proclaimed from the beginning. **Redemption by definition is to reclaim what already belongs.** Our identity is mirrored in Jesus, just as Jesus is mirrored in God. Redemption is the timeless effect of the cross for ALL mankind.

I can no longer hold on to the "chaff" I was boldly taught with passion and sincerity to believe. *Jesus did not come to establish a religion of do's, don'ts, or won'ts.* Religion has made the cross a conditional proposition based on a law of works. In other words religion would have us believe that what Jesus did on the cross was an invitation to DO something in order for an "effect" to take place in our life. This belief totally denies the finished work of Christ. **God's love is unconditional in all conditions.** God redeemed ALL mankind. You and I belong to Him from the beginning. We are His children not by choice but by birthright.

> *Redemption is the timeless effect of the cross for ALL mankind.*

Jesus died at the hands of men and women who did not know who He was, or whose they were. They were lost "sheep" crying out to the authorities, "Crucify Him" . . . their loving shepherd. Perhaps they never knew it. Being lost in the Garden of Eden or at the foot of the cross, or in the church pew, will never nullify the timeless effect of Jesus' finished work for ALL.

"For the son of man has come to
SEEK AND to SAVE that which was LOST."
(Luke 19:10 NKJV)

"All we like sheep have gone astray;
We have turned, every one, to his own way."
(Isaiah 53:6 NKJV)

Who and what was lost? These two Scriptures bring clarity to my mind. The WHO is All. ALL means ALL in any language. The WHAT is described as "Turning to his own way" as in a lost identity. Remember . . . one cannot be lost unless they first belong. Being lost does not negate belonging or value. Both facts are confirmed when the "shepherd" seeks after them with purpose and intent to find. Logic tells me that within the context of Jesus seeking and saving are these truths.

- **ALL belong and have value.**
- **ALL will be sought after.**
- **ALL will be found and saved.**

Most Religions do not argue the fact that Jesus seeks after the lost. BUT, Christianity suggests that one who chooses to remain lost by not believing, and dies in that lost condition, will not be saved. The flip side of that "coin" is that if I choose to be found . . . if I believe, then I will be saved. To me this totally contradicts logic, let alone the premise above. *Believing does not make something become true. Believing affirms what already is true.* How much more when considering the words of God. As if this is not

> *Believing does not make something become true. Believing affirms what already is true.*

contradictory enough, doctrines of eternal separation, judgment, punishment, and torment from God were added as consequences for one's choice to remain lost. This is to deny a God of Unconditional Love, and promotes a destructive dichotomy of mindsets spoken against in 1 Corinthians 13.

Paul declared there is one God and Father of all. Jesus' death on the cross was, is, and continues to be a proclamation and declaration of God's unconditional Love. From Adam to the newest life being birthed this very second, our value and belonging is declared before time began. Francois Dutoit has beautifully encapsulated this truth.

*"We were found in Christ
Before we were ever Lost in Adam."*

"Threshing and Winnowing" God's words has been the highlight of writing this book. I feel like I have been in a yoke with Jesus. Applying logic has yielded an abundant harvest. When we dare to ask, "why do I believe what I believe?" God will always meet us where we are. We will never be met with offense by God. We often do not question our beliefs because we are fearful of God's reaction. Our beliefs are so tightly woven into the fabric of our Biblical interpretations. To question our beliefs has been equated to our questioning "God's Word" . . . AKA the Bible. We will expand on this further in the next chapter. In Him we live and move and have our being. His desire is that you KNOW you have a place of belonging. You are, always have been and will always be loved and valued. You will always be FOUND in the intrinsic nature of His unconditional love, regardless of choices and subsequent consequences in behavior. I believe this was, is, and will always be His purpose and intent for all of mankind as He eternally declares . . .

"IT IS FINISHED!"

A MATTER OF SEMANTICS

To believe a lie about God will translate to a lie about yourself.

I write this chapter with humility, passion, and confidence because I have come to trust in God's unconditional love and His desire for us to know our true identity. I want the content of this chapter to have its own significance in your mind and heart, thus its unconventional 5.5 numbering. It is truly a road less traveled when taking a journey with words down the controversial path of questioning the accuracy of the Bible. One of the foundational doctrines I was taught within Christianity was the inerrancy of

> *To believe a lie about God will translate to a lie about yourself.*

Scripture. It never entered my mind to challenge my parents, pastors, Sunday school teachers or Bible school professors on this topic. I'll admit I would occasionally run into verses I didn't understand and which seemed to be contradictory to other places within Scripture. Truthfully, I felt my "teachers" did too, but tastefully gave explanations at best and ignored them at worst.

In Acts 17:11, Paul and Silas are said to have preached to Jews in Berea. We will look at Paul's testimony in chapter 13. History tells us the location of this city would have included people of non Jewish heritage, namely Greeks, who may also have been exposed to the teachings of Paul. Their response is what I want us to focus on. I love how Mitchell's Greek New Testament's rendering adds depth to this passage.

" . . . they were folks who received and welcomed the Logos (the Word; the message; the idea) with eagerness (rushing forward), repeatedly examining again, separating back and sifting up and down the Scriptures day by day to determine if these continue having it thus (holding it in this way)"

When was the last time you showed "eagerness" to look further into the preaching of God's word? When did you do your own research, "separating and sifting" the words spoken or written, taking into consideration context, culture, church history, style in writing, hyperbolic language and linguistics?

It is further recorded in History that the Bereans examined the words they heard by comparing them to the Old Testament Scriptures and conducting their own research. They did not have the 66 books of the Bible that we have today. I would logically conclude that this research included hearing the personal testimonies of those who had walked and talked with Jesus. The result was that their eyes were opened to truth, similar to those who walked the road to Emmaus. Jesus always rightly divided the Scriptures by pointing to Himself within the words, always recounting a message of love and liberty in contrast to fear and bondage.

The approach taken by these devoted men and women in studying the Scriptures is an example and model for all those who would desire to know TRUTH. The Bible is a treasure chest of life giving, life changing words of God. But just as Adam fell prey to adversarial rhetoric in his mind, so have we. World renowned Bible scholars and translators are no exception.

According to my research, most Biblical scholars agree that the literacy level in Jesus' day was 2%. This was astonishing to me. 98% were dependent on the Religious and political figures to instruct them in the ways they were to conduct their lives. As History unfolded there was no separation between church and state. Temple priests were not only religious leaders, but also served as judges and rulers. In the 4th Century when the first Bible was written, separate religious and political orders continued to lack clarity in their defined roles within most civilizations. Political unrest led to a desire for power and control over the people. Religion was a department of the state. Therefore, people worshiped the gods of the particular state in which they lived. Foreign and unfamiliar words from a plethora of paganistic beliefs found their way into later manuscripts and into our translations. They manipulated the people politically and religiously. The number one tactic of the religious teachers of the law was to use *fear* to promote compliance. It should also be noted that often words recorded as having been spoken by Jesus, would not have even been in the language/ vocabulary Jesus spoke. This is a significant point.

Remember Jesus' words, "sheep without a shepherd", when referring to the Jews? Sheep are totally dependent on their shepherd for their well being. Many people have adopted this same "sheep" mentality toward religious leaders. Sad to say, religious leaders throughout history have been "blind shepherds / guides" according to the words of Jesus in *Matthew 15:14*. To me it is a travesty that Biblical teaching and reception of words continue to be taught and believed to be completely accurate and without error. Despite the well documented mistranslations and insertions of words, pastor / teachers sincerely continue to proclaim a fear driven gospel. Please consider reading Brad Jersak's book, A More Christlike Word. It is truly inspired by God to challenge us in this very controversial matter of inerrancy. Brad is truly an example of one *who has a mind liberated in the spirit of love; a mind saved from tolerating inferior thoughts; fearless and unstoppable. (2 Timothy 1:7 Mirror Study Bible)*

With modern day technology at our fingertips and styluses, there is no logical reason to live in ignorance, naivety, and blindness. When we are unwilling to question why we believe what we believe, we risk

> *Perceptions and perspectives of men were interwoven with words from God.*

becoming impervious to truth and susceptible to lies. Literacy is a gift. Having access to resources in which we can explore words in their context of history, culture, and linguistics, lends to more accurate interpretation and translation of words.

To say that our Bibles are without error is an ancient mindset perpetrated by "blind guides". Even God made reference in the Old Testament to the "lying pens of the scribes". *(Jeremiah 8:8, 9)* This would indicate perceptions and perspectives of men were interwoven with words from God. One who would challenge the words found in their Bible is often branded a Heretic. With purpose and intent Jesus challenged the dogma of the religious leaders. He opposed their mindsets and beliefs and mishandling of the Scriptures. Jesus saw the Scriptures as all about God's plan to come to mankind in human flesh to show us His love. The treasures of God's words in the pages of the Scriptures are waiting to be discovered. They are camouflaged by doctrines of men built on mistranslations and insertion of words supported by assumptions. We have the privilege and responsibility to "dig" out the gold and "sift out the "debris".

When we read Paul's words to Timothy in *2 Timothy 3* we are faced with verses interpreted by many to suggest the Bibles we have today are without error. Verse 16 states, All scripture is inspired by God. Today we reference "ALL Scripture" in a context of a myriad of translations used to teach doctrines within over 45,000 denominations. We do not have any original manuscripts. The earliest manuscripts date back to 300-250 BC known as the Greek Septuagint. The following is taken from a post written by Francois du Toit on August 11, 2022;

> *"All our bibles use the 1000 years later Masoretic Hebrew text instead of the Septuagint Greek Old Testament."*

Why is this significant? The Greek Septuagint would have been that which was used by Jesus and the Apostle Paul. Therefore, the verse quoting Paul's words to Timothy would have been referencing the Greek Septuagint. Below is an example given by Francois in continuation of context. *(See Isaiah 54:16 in the LXX Greek Septuagint)*

"The word "NOT" makes such a difference!
Here it is from the Masoretic Hebrew text:

"I create the blacksmith who fires up his forge and makes a weapon designed
to kill.
I also create the destroyer!"

But the Septuagint Greek Old Testament 300-250 BC says,

*"Behold, I have created you, **NOT** as the coppersmith blowing coals,*
and bringing out a vessel [fit] for work;
*I have created you **NOT** for ruin*
that you should destroy or be destroyed."

This is why the Mirror Study Bible translation has become invaluable to me.

I would surmise that Paul's reference to "inspiration" was not limited to words on parchment. It is the LIVING WORD who INSPIRES. Personal testimonies [including his own] of face to face encounters with Jesus "THE WORD" gave witness to this. Paul was reminding Timothy of the life giving words he was raised with generationally.

Without a doubt, the Bible has become one of the most confusing and misunderstood pieces of literature, not to mention divisive books in the hands of men. When Jesus "opened the Scriptures" to the disciples on the Road to Emmaus, He opened their minds to understand HIS WORDS. Not only words spoken but to understand who He was in His very essence. Why is this important? When we have a distorted view of

God, we will have a distorted view of ourselves and our purpose. If words written or spoken are incongruent with the character of God, they are words of men and not words of God. We must also acknowledge that *Spirit is the only one who reveals absolute truth, opens blind eyes, and gives understanding to minds and hearts.* God will not deny himself. If words on a page contradicts God's character, they are to be challenged.

I believe we today are inspired in the same way as men of old. Many books written today give evidence of God's continued breath of life (absolute truth) being proclaimed. I have listed many of them in my acknowledgments. There are also a plethora of books written by men and women who, though having the Spirit of God within, rely on their own understandings, perspectives, and perceptions. They have not followed the example of the Bereans. I do believe Jesus, His Spirit, and the Father are the same yesterday today and forever. That makes the Gospel message the same yesterday, today, and forever. Mankind's gift to choose has not changed either. Therefore, we can choose to live in the Logic of God or with indoctrination, teaching devoid of critical thinking. Spirit will open our eyes as we rightly divide with the mind / logic of Christ. God's desire is for us to know His Heart in every circumstance of life. This to me is learning to trust in and embrace God's Love without a trace of conditions or condemnation. He is as close as our next breath. He invites us as little children to crawl up into His lap and ask any question we want. I fully believe that when we read or hear something that makes us afraid of Him, He will lovingly, and full of Grace tell us to let those words blow away like chaff in the wind of His Spirit. I envision Jesus whispering in our ear, *"They just didn't know who I AM. Let me tell you what I so passionately wanted them to know and proclaim."* Then listen. He is about to reveal to you Himself in Scripture. Jesus is the logic of God. He cannot be WHO HE IS and NOT BE WHO HE IS. Words matter, because YOU matter.

Why is the gospel message (Good News) being proclaimed today, on a foundation of fear (bad news), warning us of God's wrath? Is it any wonder that we approach God with timidity and reluctance when we come across words in our Bibles such as found in Romans 5:9? **God never intended us to live in fear. Fear and love cannot cohabitate.**

I will quote *Romans 5:9* from a Bible I have read for years, memorized, and in which I have written notes in the margins. I will follow this translation with a Greek amplified translation.

> *"Since, therefore, we have now been justified by His blood,*
> *much more shall we be saved by him from*
> ***The wrath OF GOD.****" (ESV)*

> *"Much more, then –*
> *being NOW Eschatologically delivered and rightwised;*
> *Through Him we will continue being rescued*
> *away from the conditions or situations of personal emotion,*
> *our anger and* **HUMAN WRATH."**
> *(Mitchell's Greek New Testament)*

The *wrath of God and human wrath are not one and the same.*

The ESV translation is not to be considered JUST a mistranslation. **This is a literal insertion of the words "OF GOD", not found in the manuscripts of old.** This manipulation of Scripture changed the entire meaning. The Greek rendering is in keeping with the context of Paul's writing in the book of Romans. He often spoke of our need to renew our mind. The correct interpretation of this verse tells us why and from what. Paul knew very well a mindset fueled by one's own human passions and wrath was one driven by performance and behavior based on the law. Christ's finished work of the cross (before the foundation of the world) declared all mankind righteous apart from the law of works. Mankind has lost their identity. I cannot overemphasize how important this one example is.

Jesus' purpose and intent when challenging the religious leaders' teachings was to address their misrepresenting God. By placing more emphasis on performance and compliance to the written words of law they were blind to the LIVING WORD (JESUS). By doing this, they were also living a life contradictory to LOVE. God is Love.

Religious leaders throughout history have exhibited POWER and control over people by misinterpreting the Scriptures. I think we can all agree that to LOVE and be loved is a shared desire of ALL mankind at some level in all relationships. This would include our relationship with God. It's in our DNA to desire God's approval and love. Our MIND is key in discerning words of love from words of fear.

(2 Timothy 1:7 NKJV)
"God has not given to us a Spirit of **FEAR**,
But of **POWER***, and of* **LOVE** *and of a* **SOUND MIND**.

Now let's read it in the Greek New Testament:

"God does not give to us, (or supply for us) a breath-effect or attitude of **timidity** *in us, but rather an attitude of ability and of* **power***,
as well as of* **love** *(a drive toward reunion) and of* **soundness in frame of mind***. (of wholeness in thinking; Of healthiness of attitude;
Of sanity; of sensibility")*

Do you see the meaning of "sound mind" so beautifully defined in this Greek rendering? We sacrifice true love, wholeness, mental well being, and sensibility on the altar of fear. Spirit is our teacher, not the law. Only Spirit can breathe life into us. The law kills. (See 2 Corinthians 3:6) Oh that we would fully embrace the truth that God welcomes our questions. I cannot overstate the fact that ***we will never be met with offense from God when applying LOGIC to the Scriptures.*** For too long we have given more credence to and amazement in the preservation of a book promoting performance to the law of works rather than focusing on GOD'S ETERNAL WORDS of LIFE, promoting obedience (hearing and embracing) the law of love. This is exactly what Jesus was referring to whenever he addressed the Religious leaders. They had allowed the law to become their tutor. If words written or spoken suggest judgment, wrath and

We will never find the Love of God in performance driven doctrines.

punishment from God for any reason, under any circumstances, they are not words of God. We will never find the Love of God in performance driven doctrines.

Jesus never has and never will be on a crusade to defend and protect a Book of words. We dare not make THE WORD (Jesus) synonymous with "the word of God" (Bible). Logically it makes no sense to make such a claim based on previously mentioned statistics. I suppose there are some who would argue that this is a form of semantics and I would have to agree in the purest and strongest sense of this word's definition.

> *"Semantics is the linguistics and logic*
> *concerned with meaning;*
> *the study of the meaning of words and phrases."*
> *(Oxford Languages)*

I find it ironic that the phrase, "It's just semantics," becomes a scapegoat for NOT wanting to engage in meaningful research and study of words in the Bible. This tragically includes unwillingness to participate in open dialogue, challenging us to examine the scriptures and look outside the box of our beliefs. When we refuse to practice what the very word semantics embodies by definition, our indoctrinated rhetoric drowns out the still small voice within us. In Scripture this is called *"quenching" the Spirit or "suffocating the flame of the spirit within you." (1 Thessalonians 5:19 NIV and Mirror Study Bible respectively)*

Hebrews 4:12 is a scripture commonly used within Christianity to equate the written word of God with Jesus.

"For the word of God is living and active,
sharper than any two-edged sword,
piercing to the division of soul and of spirit,
of joints and of marrow,
and discerning the thoughts and intentions of the heart" (ESV)

The only way the verbiage "word of God" can be accurately interpreted is to go back to John 1:1 and interpret those words accurately.

JESUS is the only AUTHORITATIVE WORD. HIS LIFE IS THE ONLY COMPLETELY ACCURATE INTERPRETATION and TRANSLATION!

If only we truly believed this. It would liberate us from a subconscious fear of questioning what we were told to believe and the words in the BIBLE that we were told to memorize and hide in our hearts. Within every life indwells God's Spirit . . . the very WORD OF GOD. Therefore, every life is INSPIRED.

When our mind becomes entwined with God's mind (see Philippians 2:5), we will begin to see ourselves as God sees us. We are born from above and embraced in a circle of unconditional love.

The Word of God is JESUS . . . not a Book.

"Perfect Love casts out fear." This familiar verse can be found in 1 John 4:18, but is often quoted out of context. Have you ever asked yourself . . . "Fear of what?" John makes it very clear. Please don't miss this. The text is not endorsing a performance based love relationship in order to escape a God of Judgment and wrath. On the contrary, the text endorses our secured position in the LOVE OF GOD from the beginning of time, whether we believe it or not. John was writing to dispel any belief in an expectation of judgment or wrath from God. THERE IS NO FEAR IN LOVE, GOD IS LOVE, and WE RESIDE IN HIS LOVE!

(1 John 4:18 Mirror Study Bible)
"Fear cannot co-exist in this love realm.
The perfect love union that we are talking about expels fear.
Fear holds on to an expectation of crisis and judgment
[which brings separation] and interprets it as due punishment.
It echoes torment and only registers in someone
*who does not yet realize the **completeness of their love union.**"*

I challenge you to examine why you believe what you believe. I have maintained from the very beginning of this book that words come our way and are offered for our consideration to accept or reject. Perhaps you are reading this book with preconceived beliefs and solidified mindsets regarding who God is. It becomes your choice and opportunity to process words by applying critical thinking with Logic, based on Absolutes. I'm not asking you to trust me. I am imploring you to TRUST GOD! He wants us to know TRUTH and be SET FREE. This is not an invitation to know God academically. The Word of God is JESUS . . . not a Book. This is an invitation to engage in a mutual LOVE RELATIONSHIP without fear. When fear rears its ugly head in any step in this process, you can know you have stepped out of the realm of absolute truth.

I cannot end this chapter without addressing a very destructive manipulation of Scripture within Christendom. A proverbial warning was etched in my mind in regard to questioning any words in the Bible. The following are my words to express my former mindset.

CAUTION! ENTER AT YOUR OWN RISK!
You are about to remove 'jots and tittles',
adding to or taking away from the scriptures,
which is forbidden by God.

This bit of sarcasm is not meant to offend. These, "Jots and tittles" and "adding and taking away" words found in the Bible (see Matthew 5:18), have been manipulated and taken out of context. In doing so, we have essentially been paralyzed by fear to not think for ourselves. We have perpetuated a mindset of dependency on others to tell us what to believe.

We have essentially been paralyzed by fear to not think for ourselves.

My prayer for anyone reading this book is that you no longer give in to a spirit of fear. Being enslaved to doctrines of men will prevent you from soaring the heights on eagle wings of God's UNCONDITIONAL LOVE.

Fear will keep you shackled. Love will set you FREE!

I AM . . . THEREFORE, YOU ARE

Within the greatest Love Story ever recorded in History, the Religious leaders in the time of Jesus couldn't connect the dots. It is ironic to me that GOD was literally standing in front of them, in the flesh, and they were virtually saying,

YOU ARE NOT to the "I AM."

The I AM of the Old Testament is Jesus. And Jesus in the New Testament is the I AM. So how did they not recognize Him? Obviously Jesus did not have a "resume" befitting their perceived job description for God. They disqualified Jesus as being the prophesied Messiah due to pre-programmed mindsets and beliefs about who God was.

The identity of Jesus was in question
because their perception of God was
based on a lie.

Anyone who has read even small portions of the Old Testament can agree that there is an overwhelming emphasis placed on commandments and laws; 613 to be exact. As young Jewish boys, now adult teachers of the law, they were required to memorize and adhere to thousands of words of Scripture. They had studied the prophecies regarding the coming of the Messiah and therefore were anticipating His arrival. But who or what were they expecting? Because of ongoing political tension fueled by religious ideas and expectations, there was ongoing oppression and upheaval. The Religious leaders were often caught in the middle of both arenas. They were looking for a Messiah to end this chaos. By definition the Messiah was to be a Savior, Redeemer, and King. Entwined in the minds of the religious leaders came an expected "to do list" for the Messiah as they awaited His return. They were also convinced that approval from God would be theirs if they carried out their perceived "marching orders" to obey and enforce ALL the laws and commandments. This brings us back to what was stated in Chapter 3. When we look at the mindsets of the Religious leaders, we cannot deny the importance of these questions.

"What comes into your mind
when you think about God?"
And
"What do you believe
God believes
to be true about you?"

God is Love, therefore, having been made in His image and His likeness Love indwells us. *Jesus came to planet earth to show us the I AM, not the I DO.* The "doing" or "behavior" will correspond to our choice to live in the knowledge of our union with Jesus. Lucious fruit grown on a tree does not travail or labor into being. Fruit is in the DNA of the seed. That is what image and likeness is. It is imperative that we understand WHO HE IS in order to understand WHO WE ARE!

HE IS therefore WE ARE!

Jesus came to planet earth to show us the I AM, not the I DO.

In both the Old and New Testament, Religious leaders were referred to by God and Jesus as "Blind Guides" and referred to the Jewish people as "Sheep without a Shepherd." Their IDENTITY WAS LOST. While the religious leaders were, over time, saturated in a "mist" of Scripture, those who followed their teachings found themselves lost in a thick "fog" of laws and commandments. Doctrines of men require actions on man's part to gain and remain in an eternal and secure love relationship with God. This approach will always be accompanied by expectations to comply, motivated by fear. Jesus came to show us His Love relationship with His Father, thus revealing God's love relationship with us. Our Identity is secure because of God's love, not based on good behavior.

(1 John 4:16,18 Mirror Study Bible)
Vs. 16 "We have come to know and believe the love that
God has unveiled within us. God is Love. Love is who God is;
To live in this place of conscious, constant love, is to live immersed in God
and feel perfectly at home in His indwelling."

Vs. 18 "Fear cannot co-exist in this love realm. The Perfect love union that
we are talking about expels fear. Fear holds on to an expectation of crisis and
judgment and interprets it as due punishment.
It echoes torment and only registers in someone who does not yet realize the
completeness of their love union with the Father, Son and Spirit
and with one another."

Fear, guilt, and shame can only thrive in an environment of expectations and conditions. The mindset of God's love being conditional has been sewn into the fabric of all religions. I found it to be true in Christiantiy. When clothed in a garment of sin consciousness, our true identity becomes camouflaged. The result is that we no longer see ourselves as God sees us.

God's Identity became our identity because of the Finished work of Jesus. All of mankind are clothed in the beautiful garment of Christ's Righteousness. The fabric of our being is a beautiful tapestry. Regardless of our behavior, God's never ending, unconditional love is embroidered into our DNA. God weaves even the dark threads of unbelief and poor choices in our lives in ways to never distract from the strands of gold and silver. Rainbows always look brightest when contrasted with dark skies. God wastes nothing in our lives.

> *"There is only one God.*
> *He remains the ultimate Father of the Universe.*
> *We are because He is. He is present in all;*
> *He is above all, through all, and in all."*
> *(Ephesians 4:6 Mirror Study Bible)*

Religion has misconstrued the purpose and intent of the incarnation and the culmination of the cross. Jesus was not giving an invitation to "receive or reject" a gift of becoming righteous based on our behavior. He was making a proclamation that ALL mankind are declared Righteous from the beginning. We were clothed in a garment of righteousness when God placed us in His never ending unconditional love relationship. We are sons and daughters by birthright, not by choice. This is our identity.

> *"He rescued the integrity of our original design and revealed that we have always been His own from the beginning, even before time was. This has nothing to do with anything we did to qualify or disqualify ourselves. We are not talking about religious good works or Karma here. Jesus unveils grace to be the eternal intent of God! Grace celebrates our precreation innocence and now declares our redeemed union with God in Christ Jesus." (2 Timothy 1:9 Mirror Study Bible)*

> *"He associated us in Christ before the fall of the world!* **Jesus is God's mind made up about us!** *He always knew in His love that he would present us again face-to-face before Him in blameless innocence."*
> *(Ephesians 1:4 Mirror Study Bible)*

So I ask you, where are your accusers? Jesus' words: *"On that day, you will know that we are in seamless union with one another! I am IN my Father, you are IN me and I AM IN YOU!"*

Jesus was not giving an invitation. He was making a proclamation.

**"It is not our knowing (believing) that
positions Jesus in the Father or us in Him
or the Spirit of Christ in us!
Our knowing (believing) simply awakens us
to the reality of our redeemed oneness!"**
(verse and accompanying commentary note on John 14:20 Mirror Study Bible)

In Acts 17:28 (ESV), Paul speaks these words to his audience:

"In Him, (Jesus), WE live and move and have our being. As even some of your poets have said, 'For we are indeed His offspring.' " This is a fascinating passage. Who was Paul speaking to when he used the word WE? Paul is making the statement, so logically he is a part of the "we."

In this context Paul was addressing Greek Philosophers . . . not Christians. If anything, they were pagan worshipers of many gods and *he was giving them a lesson on their IDENTITY, the absolute truth of their origin.* Paul did not preface his statement of their being idol worshipers with any conditions to become anything. You see, their upbringing in philosophy and paganism, and subsequent mindsets and behaviors, did not nullify the Absolute truth of their origin. These pagans were GOD'S OFFSPRING in spite of their practices. If this is a foreign mindset and belief to you, please take the time to consider asking yourself why you believe otherwise. John 1:12 has always been a "go to" verse to support a doctrine of "us and them," the righteous and unrighteous, the believer and the unbeliever.

> *"Everyone who realizes their association in Him,*
> *convinced that he is their original life,*
> *and that his name defines them,*
> *God **gives** the assurance that they are indeed his offspring,*
> *Begotten of him; he sanctions the legitimacy of their sonship."*
> (John 1:12 Mirror Study Bible)

The word gives is crucial to correctly interpret and understand the message of John in these verses. Please ponder the Greek meaning of this word in its context.

> *"God gives, *didomi*, in this case to give something to some*
> *one that already belongs to them; thus, to return. The fact that they already*
> *are his own, born from above and that they have their beginning and their*
> *being in Him is now confirmed in their realizing it!"*
> (Commentary note Mirror Study Bible)

Believing is realizing the truth that is. Throughout Scripture the word "believe" is given an inseparable relationship with the word "saved". Saved from what? Regrettably man's doctrine of salvation has given the word "saved" a context in which one who is not saved is an unbeliever, and will be eternally separated from God in hell. To assume one's belief "saves" them from a place of everlasting torment not only ignores context, it also ignores the very core meaning of the word "believe". If the Gospel preached to you today includes a message of fear and separation from God in any context, it is a "DIFFERENT GOSPEL" Paul speaks of in Galatians 1:6-7.

> *(vs 6) "I am amazed that you can so easily be fooled*
> *into swapping the Gospel for a gimmick.*
> *The Gospel reveals the Integrity of your original identity*
> *rescued in Christ;*

The gimmick is a Conglomeration of Grace and legalism.
This mixture boils down to a do-it-yourself plan of salvation."
(vs 7) "There is no other gospel in spite of the many so-called Christian
products branded "gospel." If any hint of the law remains,
it is not good news but merely religious people's ideas,
detracting from the gospel of Christ."

Lloyd and I can say from the bottom of our hearts, "the Love of God compels us." When we discerned the difference between the doctrines of men and the Absolute Truth of God's words, we were able to see ourselves and ALL of mankind as God sees us. We are even able to genuinely love those who have ridiculed and shunned us. In John 9:1-12 we read the account of a blind man, who had an encounter with Jesus and his sight was restored. I love Jesus' response to a question asked by His disciples when approaching this man who is known to be blind from birth.

(Vs. 2) " . . . Master, whose sin is responsible for this man's condition; Is he punished for his own sins, or perhaps for his parent's sins? Why was he born blind?" (vs.3) "Jesus answered emphatically, 'His condition has absolutely nothing to do with any sins committed either by himself or his parents. Neither him nor his parents were guilty of sin. This is an opportunity for God's action in Christ to be unveiled in him." (vs 6) . . . "He spat on the ground and made clay with the spittle; then he anointed the eyes of the blind man with the clay." "And Jesus said unto him, 'Go, and wash in the pool of Siloam.' . . . The man went there and washed and returned, Seeing perfectly."

Have you ever wondered if the blind man would have been cured of his blindness if He had not washed the mud off his eyes? God could have spoken the word, SEE, and it would have been so. I can only conclude that the blind man's participation was as necessary as Jesus' words. For me, the clay represented the law driven message of works which continually attempts to dowse the light. Neither my husband nor I were born physically blind, but our minds became darkened to the truth because of what we were sincerely taught to believe. Have you ever forgotten to remove sunglasses from your face after having been in bright light? You had diminished the light of day and then proceeded to enter a well lit room and wondered why everyone and everything looked dark. Remaining in darkness became a choice at that moment. You could have continued to leave the dark glasses on, ignoring both the affect and effect of the glasses. Or you could come to your senses and remove the glasses. Spirit within desires we come to our senses and choose to remove that which is causing the darkness. Darkness will never extinguish the light, but our choices may obscure the light.

We must not confuse participation with work. An example of work in the above analogy, would be to turn on more lights in the well lit room while keeping our dark glasses on. Participation is to enter into the room, take off the dark glasses and acknowledge the lights already on. *Taking off the glasses did not produce the light, it revealed it.*

This story in John 9 is a beautiful illustration of Jesus' identity as the light, and man's identity, the flawless cut diamond reflecting the light. Our identity will always reveal God's faith entwined with our faith with an immediate effect of SIGHT and LIGHT.

"Your salvation is not a reward for good behavior! It was a grace thing from start to finish; you had no hand in it. Even the gift to believe simply reflects His faith! BY GRACE YOU ARE, having been saved by the gift of faith; grace reveals who we are and the faith of God persuades us of it. It was God's faith to begin with. Jesus is both the source and conclusion of faith." (Ephesians 2:8 (Mirror Study Bible)

Allow me to close with this conclusion. God's faith, love, grace, and mercy have no time constraints or conditions. He is I AM . . . not I was or I will be. In contrast, man operates within time constraints, resulting in segregated mindsets filled with expectations and conditions placed on oneself and others. The most ambiguous time constraint is that which separates physical life from physical death. There is much debate over what takes place after physical death based on decisions made prior to death. In the minds of men impending death has become a culmination of time constraints. Within doctrinal beliefs, imposed mandates not met in this life, will have serious consequences after death, especially those supposedly imposed by God.

Darkness will never extinguish the light, but our choices may obscure the light.

This belief is contrary to the Logic of God. His purpose and intent from the beginning has never changed. For us to choose life is to experience the truth of our origin in His "I AMness" in eternity past, present and future. To believe otherwise is to live in a lost identity with fear of perceived separation from God in death for all eternity. We may choose to live as though dead, but in reality we never have been nor will be separated from God. Eternal life is not a segment in time after death as I was raised to believe. Jesus made this clear. He gives His definition of **Eternal life** in His prayer recorded in John 17:3:

*"**Now this is eternal life** . . . to progressively come to intimately and experientially know God and Jesus Christ." (Mitchell's Greek New Testament)*

" . . . to engage in the inexhaustible adventure of knowing you, the only true God and Jesus as the Christ whom you have commissioned! . . . should keep on knowing." (Mirror Study Bible)

Our participation in receiving sight is timeless. It is not a "work" to perform in life to someday receive a reward thereby escaping a place of eternal darkness and separation from God. His Unconditional love, grace, and mercy are timeless because Jesus is the author and finisher of faith. *KNOWING* we are included in His righteousness *IS TO LIVE in the faith of God.*

"Herein lies the secret of the power of the Gospel; there is no good news in it until the righteousness of God is revealed. The dynamic of the gospel is the revelation of God's faith as the only valid basis for our belief."

(Romans 1: 17 Mirror Study Bible)

In Jesus there is no darkness. *The only darkness we will ever experience is in the blindness within our own minds.* Once we acknowledge our blindness, and participate in the logic of God's words, we will walk in light. I liken this to washing off the clay in the pool of Siloam.

"To walk in the light as He is in the light means to see your life and everything that concerns you, exclusively from your Father's point of view. To live a life consistent with the life of our design."
(1 John 1:7 Mirror Study Bible)

The only darkness we will ever experience is in the blindness within our own minds.

The reality of consequences from choices we or others in our life have made in our blindness, can lead to woundedness and brokenness. Fear and regrets can keep our minds and hearts in the shadows, dousing the light and dulling the senses. Living life "consistent with the life of our design" is to believe in God's unconditional love.

Shadows will come, but we can choose to move out of the shadows and into the light of God's love.

A View of God's Character from An Ancient Hebrew 4 Letter word

There was no greater source of motivation for writing this book than my own journey through the pain of rejection. As I share, I want to remain true to my purpose and intent. That is to choose life giving words which align our minds and hearts with God's Character of love, even and especially in our woundedness and brokenness. Paul Hegstrom is the author of the book, "Broken Children, Grown up Pain." As he develops his premise, based on years of research, he gives us a list of causes for such emotional pain. **Rejection** is at the top of that list. There are many forms of Rejection but one in particular stands out in our family's history . . . **divorce**. When my first husband and I started anticipating marriage, I clearly remember we affirmed that divorce would never be an option after we said, "I do." To me this was based more on our mutual law driven religious upbringing and Biblical training than on a firm understanding of God's Unconditional love.

Grievously, by no choice of mine, our 6 children and I became victims of divorce. My heart has always struggled with the fact that it takes two to say "I do" but only one to say, "I'm done". Truth be known, even my husband fell victim to the consequences of divorce. Sadly, the reality of children feeling rejected when parents divorce is often ignored or denied. It doesn't

Rejection is the antithesis to God's Character of unconditional love.

matter how often you tell a child they are loved, when in the same breath they are being told their Mom and Dad no longer love each other. Children feel torn apart and often carry a sense of helplessness in being unable to stop the process. On more than one occasion our youngest son, now with children of his own, through tears has said these words . . . "if only I could have" . . . and "I should have tried to stop it." I repeatedly assured him of his innocence then and now. Children will experience woundedness and brokenness unique to their age and individuality. Separation, though necessary at times, can potentially undermine the truth of God's inseparable Love. However, rejection is the antithesis to God's Character of unconditional love, causing deep woundedness and brokenness.

The Apostle Paul reminds us in Romans 8:35-39 that Nothing can or will separate us from His love. Though sometimes difficult to process, God's heart expressed here is for both the one being rejected and the one initiating the rejection. Truth be known, in most cases, if not all, the rejector has been a victim of rejection as well. That is a key statement as I continue to write.

In chapter two I made this statement. Acceptance or rejection are two broad categories in which implied or perceived words will fall into. The most important choice our mind has to make is to align these words with either absolute truth or relative truth. Our feeling loved or fearful, included or separated, valued or worthless, will hang in the balance depending on that choice. Divorce often becomes a choice when words and behaviors contradict the character of God. Identity is the motivation behind words. When we lose sight of the truth of who God says we are, our words and behavior reflect a performance based mindset. We experience disappointment in ourselves or others due to unmet expectations resulting in guilt, and shame. This often leads to fear. I have lived in this quagmire of emotions.

While navigating through such uncharted waters of divorce, I was surrounded by loving family and friends who gave me much wanted and needed support. The Love I experienced came in many forms for which I will be forever grateful. With that being said, I was also met with deeply rooted doctrines and opinions. Strong emotions and unwavering beliefs are often a reflection of the ripple effect of woundedness and brokenness.

For centuries diverse and personal beliefs with regard to divorce, were the result of mindsets formulated within doctrinal controversy on this subject. I want to be clear. My purpose in sharing my research on this topic is not to focus on relative truth. My intent is to establish a well grounded understanding of God's view on such matters of the heart. The absolute truth of God's character of unconditional love is the context from which we will see His perspective.

Divorce is deeply woven into the fabric of Scripture.

Divorce is deeply woven into the fabric of Scripture. The word appears 25 times in our Bibles. You can find it in both the Old and the New Testaments. This may not seem significant, but to me it has become leaven/yeast within the pages of Scripture so often referred to as the "bread of life". A subliminal message of separation and rejection has become chaff mixed with wheat yielding a harvest of confusion when considering God's character. This is why I want to take a look at this word divorce, from the perspective of its definition. Have you ever researched the word? One could literally spend hours on the subjects of marriage and divorce and find a plethora of laws, and practices within cultures and religions. It is a word that has always been associated with the dissolution of relationships in any society throughout History. Given the well documented inequality between men and women in the cultures of BC and AD, I can say with certainty, divorce is a man made law in the truest sense of its origin. Women were considered to be "property" or a "possession," having no voice in the legal system. They lived under strict laws of sexual behavior while often being exploited and subsequently accused of adultery, punishable to the death by stoning. Because adultery was the most common justification and rationalization for the dissolution of marriage, men would claim grounds for divorce with no accountability for their own participation in the act.

Another point to be made is this. In Scripture you will find the word divorce used allegorically when speaking of the relationship between God and the nation of Israel. It was considered an act of "adultery" or "unfaithfulness" when Israel sinned against God. When the law stated that adultery was punishable by stoning, one would conclude that God would also severely punish Israel for her "sin of adultery".

Allow me to make a conjecture based on the linguistic origin of the word Divorce. It is from the Latin word "divortium" meaning **separation**. It is also equivalent to the words "divort" or "divortere" meaning **to turn to a different way.** It is my opinion that divorce became a platform on which to develop and endorse a fear based religion of separation and rejection from God whenever we disobey Him. This included an eternal separation in Hell for those unwilling to comply with conditions required in order to receive His unconditional love. Does that even make sense?

To further support my premise, let me introduce to you the Ancient Hebrew, 4 letter word alluded to in the title of this chapter. You will find it in bold print below. The entire quotation is recorded in Malachi 2:16, and is often quoted in counseling sessions or sermons in context to God's view on the subject. Undeniable and variable doctrines have been built upon these 3 words. Man's interpretation of God's view on divorce put the "fear of God" in me. My heart's desire has always been to be "obedient to His will." For me this was not a fear of judgment from God but rather fear of His disappointment in me. Sadly, many do fear the judgment and wrath of God when facing a decision of divorce. Even though not by my choice, I was now a divorced woman. I felt a sense of responsibility for this outcome in my marriage. I felt wounded, broken, and lost.

"GOD **HATES** DIVORCE!"

It is important to note that the word HATE has been grossly mishandled. It is another example that how and why words are interpreted and used in Scripture really does matter. We have seen how God's character has been distorted when words are misused, mistranslated, or inserted into Scripture. To me, these words spoken by God have been placed alongside a list of what I call the "non-negotiable" commandments of God. Under the law, disobedience to any of God's "Thou shalt NOT" word list would result in consequences from Him. It could also potentially lead to a form of discipline and even punishment from His "appointed and anointed" religious teachers of the law. ie: your Pastor, Priest, Rabbi, or Clergy. An example of the latter would be the position held in many religious groups that anyone who has been previously divorced, is not permitted to serve in any leadership role within the church.

Hate is a very strong word, evoking a torrent of emotions in both the sender and receiver. In this context, God's character could potentially be in question. Hatred would be contradictory to His character of love. With that being said, one could easily fall into the trap of self righteousness and justification for one's hate toward another. After all . . . how could it be wrong to hate something God hates? By adopting a warped view of God's character, rejecting and shunning those who are breaking God's commandments perpetuates the man-made doctrine of separation, rejection, and abandonment by God.

In our English use of the word, hate stands in stark contrast and contradiction to the word love. My mind and heart struggled with the dichotomy of these two words. I knew that God would never contradict

His character of Love. How then could such a word be part of His vocabulary? To me God was exhibiting extreme disdain and judgment not only for the behavior, but also toward the person. Can you see the domino effect in doctrinal beliefs encompassing separation? I was raised with such beliefs. I have also heard the expression, "Hate the sin, but love the sinner." How's that going, NOT working for you? When hate toward behavior enters into our mind and heart, it is rarely separated from feelings expressed toward the one exhibiting such behavior.

In the devastating aftermath of my husband filing for divorce, I was not only dealing with the pain of rejection, I was also experiencing the mental gymnastics of guilt, shame, and severe self condemnation. What could I have done differently? What did I do to cause such reactive and extreme behavior in my husband? And worse, how could I have been so naive as to have missed the warning signals? I had become a participant in a consequence, seemingly so out of my control, that resulted in the wounding of my husband, myself, and my children. My heart was broken.

Most everyone holds to the belief that Divorce is never one sided. More important to me was, did God take that perspective as well? Was He displeased with me? How did others view me now that I was divorced? I literally cried out to God, asking Him to forgive me for everything I had done to displease my husband. *In reality, I was living in a mindset of sin consciousness and belief in a God of conditional love, not in the absolute truth of God's unconditional love.* My heart was in turmoil because my mind was indoctrinated with fear. I finally came to the understanding that the opposite of Love is not Hate. The opposite of Love is fear.

Fast forward about 10 years. I can say from the very core of my being that by this time I had learned to be content being ONE. It became my resolve, "If two can't be better than one, I will remain ONE." Yes, I desired to have a "second chance" to find the joy of love, but once again I was met with emotions connected with Doctrines of men. I really began to struggle with the doctrines of REMARRIAGE. This topic goes hand in glove with divorce. I began to read books on the subject and sought counsel from pastors and teachers, only to be met with theologians on both sides of the

> *Knowing God's heart has become even more valuable to me than time for healing.*

fence. Was I free to remarry or not? There were Bible verses interpreted, claiming to substantiate both points of view. One fact was for sure, I didn't want to disappoint God by making a decision He would be displeased with. This just added to my confusion and fear. I was literally in mental anguish. Through tears I cried out to the Lord for His Heart. I was not yet in my present understanding of God's Unconditional Love. As I look back on these years I am amazed at how God guided me with what understanding I did have, always meeting me where I was. "Time" is a gift in the process of healing. Knowing God's heart has become even more valuable to me than time for healing. It is essential for moving on from woundedness and brokenness.

This article by Doug Hershy affirms the imperative need and reason for Logic and Semantics. We must Rightly divide truth from lies when it comes to well ingrained doctrines of men. His information validates my purpose and intent to convey that words matter.

"The ancient Hebrew language is unique in how its letters and words communicate. Centuries before the common Hebrew block script used today was formed, the language began as a type of pictographic script. This script communicated in shapes and pictures that were its letters, giving each individual letter its own meaning. As these letters formed root words, the meaning of these letters were often found in the meaning of the root words that they spelled. Then the meaning of the root word is then connected to the meaning of any words that are formed from the root.

While researchers admit there is a lot they don't understand about this, no other language on earth communicates this way. And it's the original language of two thirds of the Bible. Today, our western view of hate as defined by Merriam-Webster is a very strong feeling of dislike; intense hostility. Yet the ancient Hebrew suggests something different. "Sane" (saw-nay') is the Hebrew word that is often translated as hate. The ancient pictographic letters for "sane" are a thorn and a seed. The Ancient Hebrew Lexicon of the Bible explains this: The pictograph is a picture of a thorn, then is a picture of seed. Combined, these mean "thorn seed." The thorn, (the seed of a plant with small sharp points) causes one to turn directions to avoid them. ("The Ancient Hebrew Lexicon of the Bible," by Jeff A. Benner. ISBN 1-58939-776-2.)"

*"In Biblical times, thorns were used as fences to protect flocks from predators or even used as weapons. The idea was that thorns caused pain and the pain made someone avoid whatever caused it. While intense emotions are sometimes involved, **the ancient Hebrew view of HATE was more about being hurt or wounded by something . . . then, staying away from that pain source.** Hatred was less about an intense confrontational emotion and more about making choices to avoid physical and emotional pain. **This understanding can directly affect our view of God's character."***

> *The manmade doctrines which erode God's character of love will only lead to destruction.*

This affirms the danger in using words originating from a different language and culture, and applying one's own understanding and meaning from their familiar vernacular. This would also include the application of emotional expressions not associated with that word's culture and origin. Do you see why the author of this article would suggest God's Character could be in question? I absolutely can. ***Man's law-driven use of the word divorce,** in combination with a mistranslated word used by God, **has undermined God's character.** Applying semantics to this ancient Hebraic 4 letter word HATE, changed my perspective on God's view on Divorce. Separation, rejection, and abandonment are recognized as potential sources of pain in the context of God's character of unconditional love. He does not want to see us suffer the consequences of choices we make, which are in fact a betrayal to our identity. Perhaps even more importantly God does not want our perception of His character of Love to be challenged, nor our relationship compromised because of sin consciousness and fear of His rejection and condemnation of us.

Looking back I see so clearly how I was raised in a law driven, performance based environment fostered within the church. I tragically adopted a belief of "shunning" those who strayed from God's commandments. Believing adultery and divorce were at the top of God's "hate" list, I truly thought I was doing no less than what Jesus would do. I applied a destructive behaviorally driven mindset toward my husband for his "sin" of adultery and divorcing me after 20 years of marriage. I even had Bible verses to support my position. If only I had understood not only the word HATE, but more importantly the word, sin. That word will be discussed in chapter 14. I had a distorted view of God's character which gave me a distorted view of myself and my husband. It breaks my heart to look back on similar reactions toward my children's disobedience in childhood and on into their adulthood due to a performance driven mindset. Through tears my oldest daughter shared the brokenness she experienced when she had made choices leading to adultery and divorce. Devastated by her own sin consciousness while being met with my self righteous rejection, caused her to have thoughts of suicide. *The manmade doctrines which erode God's character of love will only lead to destruction.* I cannot speak for my children. I can only give testimony to the fact that when I was faithless, He remained faithful. The Scriptures bear witness to the fact that His mercies are new every morning. Great is His faithfulness. All of our children have a relationship with Jesus and give open and verbal testimony to God's sustaining love throughout their lives, despite my "blindness". Each one's canvas is still on the loom with knots and tangled dark threads of wounds and brokenness noticeable on the underside of their tapestry. What a joy it is to focus on the beautiful art work of God's skillful weaving of ALL colors, bright and dark on the upper side. God uses it all for His Glory.

I cherish in my heart the relationship I have today with each of our 6 children. They have shared their joys and sorrows, unique to each one's tapestry of life. This Mama's heart has shed many a tear over the wounds still in need of Jesus healing balm, and the struggles in fractured and splintered relationships from past choices made. I rejoice in the fact that they are walking in the light being revealed to them right where they are in each step of their journey.

Separation has existed within human relationships since the fall of Adam, and has long since infiltrated doctrines of men. It has manifested itself in self righteous mindsets, beliefs, and behavior demonstrating a warped identity. When we know the heart of God, we can align our mind with His mind and our Heart with His heart. Will there be outbursts of anger with hurtful words said toward one another? Probably. But, when we are able to recognize words and/or behaviors that are contrary to God's Character of unconditional love, we can see them for what they are. They become "thorns" suggestive of potential harm that God wants us to avoid. We can then respond accordingly with more clarity and compassion. Choices made will be based on an absolute truth of God's love for you in avoiding harmful influences physically and emotionally. Strangely enough this mindset will acknowledge the absolute truth that God will also show His love to the one causing the pain. If one's identity is built on a foundation of love, rather than fear, we will be able to see ourselves and the one hurting us as God does. We can then avoid the self-righteous judgemental and condemnatory reactions not found in God's character of love.

God hates Divorce in the purest definition of this 4 letter word, and clearly warns against it because of the pain and suffering it causes. BUT . . . God's love prevails over ALL our choices. Both the rejector and the one being rejected are equally loved unconditionally.

Are there times physical separation is necessary in earthly relationships? Absolutely! In this there is no doubt. When sorrow and pain begin to overwhelm you, know this. God sees the end from the beginning before you were even in the throes of rejection. God enters into a broken relationship with no

> *All manmade doctrines are "thorns" to avoid.*

attention given to "who started it." He is mindful of one thing and that is your need for unconditional love. I know this from experience.

I wish to close this chapter with this very important statement. All man made doctrines are "thorns" to avoid. Words found in Scripture which contradict God's character of Love and the blueprint of our design, are a potential source of woundedness and brokenness. *"In Him we live and move and have our being."* If we should wander off into dangerous territory with "thorn seeds", and become separated in our minds in any relational encounter, God's presence is there. We will never be separated from His Love under any circumstances or consequences. Perhaps you are a victim of the effect of rejection and lost identity in someone else's life. I want to remind you that He will never abandon you. He is in your woundedness and brokenness. No matter what you have gone through or currently going through, dare to believe God's words of love and life not only for you, but also for the one who has hurt you.

Today I am no longer plagued with seeming contradictions within Scripture. The effect of painting with a broader brush on the canvas of my mind regarding issues discussed in this chapter, have been life changing. Since Lloyd's and my "road to Emmaus experience", we have continued to seek God's heart on words found in Scripture. We have applied logic to what we were taught. Researching words semantically and linguistically have resulted in an allegorical explosion of color and clarity. When we dared to question what we believed, we experienced our hearts rejoicing in the absolute truth revealed to us by God's Spirit of Love within us. I can assure you we were never met with offense from God in the process. Jesus and I continue to have creative days in the art gallery of my mind. I pray that in some small way my story portrayed in the next 3 chapters will encourage you in your journey. I am trusting you will hear God's Spirit within you.

GENERATIONAL WOUNDS
FROM CHILDHOOD BROKENNESS

When looking at our past we are faced with choices in the present which will impact our future. In this chapter I've included a glimpse into the tapestry of my childhood while weaving in threads of my parents' lives. I also am including a brief account of my first Husband's upbringing. All indicated quotations are taken from either written documentation or open conversations shared publicly.

As an only child, my Mom was the recipient of love and attention from both parents. She shared with us that she loved her Daddy very much. As a girl she loved to "play secretary" in his office. One day she began to notice that "something was going on between him and his bookkeeper." She tried to tell her Mom but, in her words, "She wouldn't listen." One night he came home, "late, ugly, and probably drunk." She further disclosed that her parents had an argument which led to his leaving and never returning. My Mom's last conversation with her Daddy was by phone, telling him that she had a high school graduation picture for him. He never connected with her to receive that picture and she never heard his voice again.

> *When looking at our past we are faced with choices in the present which will impact our future.*

After some time, my Grandmother remarried. This man was the only Grandpa my sisters and I knew. Looking back I can now say, he was verbally abusive and narcissistic in his behavior toward her. Mom told me that she never did establish a close relationship with him, but was glad that her Mother was no longer alone, and had someone to look after her. Mom saw this as her opportunity to leave home. As a young woman of 23, she was inducted into the Navy as a Wave. It was there she met my Dad, a handsome young sailor. Here is the rest of the story in her own words:

"I met your Daddy in Washington, D.C. Our barracks were right on the Potomac River, down the street from the Lincoln Monument. My shipmate asked me to go to a dance with her at the mess hall and I did. I no sooner entered the dance hall than Daddy asked me to dance. (I have never been to a dance since.) He was very interesting to talk to and treated me like a lady. He told me he played the ukulele and offered to go get his. The dance was at the mess hall in between the two barracks. My shipmates and I had always agreed not to leave a dance. Even though I trusted him, I still told my friend Kitty that we were going down to the Reflection Pool (right behind the mess hall). This was so, if I yelled for help, she could respond. It was October 12th, 1949, with a full moon shining on the water as he sang, "Shine on Harvest Moon." It was instant love. I had always vowed that I would never "go steady," but when he asked me 9 days later, I said, "YES."

⚬⚬⚬

Perceptions of who he was, manifested in beliefs contrary to what God believed to be true about him.

We know as much about our Daddy's childhood as having a puzzle with several pieces missing. He had only a Jr. High education but was a self taught man, gifted musically, and an artist in his own right. He too was an only child. My Mom told us that he was raised by his Mother, never knowing his biological Father. At age 17, while filing for his birth certificate, "he found out by accident that he was an illegitimate child." In that era, this represented a shameful family dynamic. She said he was always embarrassed about this and never talked about it. This was a burden he never should have carried alone, but chose to do so. To this day, no one knows what had been disclosed in words spoken or unspoken. One thing is sure. Perceptions of who he was, manifested in beliefs contrary to what God believed to be true about him. He slipped into eternity never experiencing such love and therefore never dealing with the pain of rejection in childhood.

Have you ever asked yourself, what does a loving family look like anyway? Think about it! Television programming in the 50's would often be a source of various versions of "normal" functioning family life. Father's were often portrayed as going to work in the morning, dressed in a suit and tie, briefcase in hand. The perfect wife was dressed in a crisply ironed cotton dress with a pearl necklace, makeup and hair flawlessly done, kissing him as he left. Often two children, usually a girl and a boy, (the "perfect" number of children and genders) came running down the stairs heading out the door to school. Mother would hand them their lunches, the dog and or cat never barking or scratching the furniture.

In stark contrast to the above scenario, there were sitcoms like, "The Honeymooners". Viewers could relate to Ralphs and Alice's constant bickering and slandering as evidenced by the laughter in the studio . . . or for that matter in one's own living room. Strangely enough, their love for one another was rarely questioned. Here is an interesting piece of trivia. The Theme music for this show was entitled, "You're my Greatest Love." You sure wouldn't surmise that from the majority of the script.

To be honest, this second example above was a closer depiction of the "Love" displayed in our home with one exception. I never heard a snide remark from Mom (as from Alice in the sitcom) toward my Daddy's hurtful words. Being "submissive" was a familiar mindset from her upbringing. My siblings and I knew she often kept silent to keep the peace in our home. By example, I learned to do the same in my first marriage.

We were a close knit family, partially due to the fact that our parents were "only" children. My 4 sisters and I had no Aunts, Uncles, or Cousins. Despite limited displays of affection, we knew that they loved each other and that we were loved. Looking back, hugs and kisses were limited to our bedtime regime, or upon returning from a time apart. We rarely saw our parents embrace each other, kiss, or even sit together. I cannot recall endearing words being spoken to one another. This became my perception of love.

There were not many occasions when we were separated from our parents. We occasionally went to our grandparent's home for a weekend, and maybe once or twice to summer camp. In these times, after the sun went down, we were homesick to the point of tears. We missed the love and security of our home.

Daddy was very protective of his 5 daughters, and voiced strong opposition to our participation in any event which could threaten our well being. This included riding roller coasters at the amusement park, participating in sports events, and most definitely riding motorcycles. Mom supported these restrictions. I guess you could say we lived a pretty sheltered life.

The seas of marriage got pretty rocky at times. In my earlier childhood I can remember Mom slamming cupboard doors, sometimes grabbing pots and pans causing a sound which could be heard far and wide. During these times we girls would see tears running down her face. Our childish lack of obedience and insensitivity to her needs, along with poor financial choices made by Daddy, certainly contributed to these occasional outbursts. We were too young to know what was really going on in her mind and heart. As I look back, It is my belief that there were unspoken words my Mom so desperately needed to hear, which fostered loneliness.

My Daddy was a hard working, proud janitor during most of my growing up years. There was also a season when he drove a school bus for our district, and my sisters and I got to tag along. He took this job seriously and enforced safety rules on every child as though they were his own. He would even stop the bus if he saw horseplay going on in his rear view mirror. If the glimpse of his stern glaring look in that large mirror did not get their attention, his 6' 4" frame marching down the bus aisle usually took care of the problem. His powerful voice would echo throughout the bus, "SIT DOWN". My sister's and I were never frightened by his reaction, nor caught by surprise to witness such an event.

Going on any family road trips would often bring out Daddy's insensitivity towards Mom with words of accusation and blame when missing a turn, or freeway entrance. "Getting us lost" was never his fault. Mom would take it in stride and sometimes chuckle. He would settle down (more or less), once we navigated onto the right road. I never remember Mom retaliating outwardly toward his hurtful words. Nor do I remember

There were unspoken words my Mom so desperately needed to hear, which fostered loneliness.

his apologizing or taking any responsibility. It is my conjecture that she would internalize for her children's sake. Not reacting was certainly a way to insure our anticipated family fun. It saddens me that she was most likely wounded in the process.

When we were in grammar school, my Daddy's janitorial job didn't bring in enough money to manage the household. Mom was forced to go to work as a Nurse's Aide on the night shift in our local hospital. She would have to leave the house before his swing shift was over. We only had one vehicle so she would leave in the dark, early enough to walk the distance to catch a bus. There was a very small gap of time when we girls were alone until he returned home. Times were different then. Doors were locked and we were safe. Looking back as a Mom myself, this had to have pulled at her heart strings.

One day, during my teenage years, Daddy left the janitorial job. Having always been enamored with the circus as a child, he decided to make a career change and become a Professional Clown. You can only imagine how interesting our life became. Balloon animals along with "magic" equipment, became our living room, and dining room decor. His stage name became "Tiny the Musical, Magical Clown". His 6'4" stature with size 13 triple D clown shoes combined with his Emmettt Kelly style face, definitely made him stand out in any crowd. He carried a guitar case from which he would pull out a tenor size ukulele. This would always bring smiles and laughter from the crowd. He was very much at home with an audience, be it at a Birthday party, Shopping Mall Grand Opening, or Corporate office Picnic event. He was loved by all.

It meant the world to him to bring a smile to a child's face when creating a balloon sculpture. He would bend over to reach their level, placing the requested balloon animal into their anxiously awaiting little hands. There were times a child would cry when they saw his clown face and I remember the demeanor of rejection he displayed, though subtle, as though he had failed. At times I would notice his expression change to disdain when older children would mock him. He always remained controlled, but it was obvious that the pain of rejection in his mind and heart was not far from the surface. You may be familiar with the phrase, "laughing on the outside, crying on the inside". Truth be known, behind that painted face, Daddy was far from being filled with joy and laughter. Looking back I can see more clearly how isolated he had become.

For many years Daddy also enjoyed a hobby which preoccupied his time when not entertaining. He was a Ham radio operator. For those of you who may be familiar with this avocation, his "call letters" were W1JCR. He would proudly "surf" the radio waves by voice or morse code identifying himself with these words. "This is W1JCR . . . Jim Chases Rabbits." This was a fitting "handle" for his

Behind that painted face, Daddy was far from being filled with joy and laughter.

career as a Professional Clown. He enjoyed his virtual encounters with fellow hams around the world, collecting hundreds of QSL cards. These were personally designed postcards with their allocated letters and numbers across the front. They became trophies well deserved for hours spent in communication world wide. Daddy's successful contacts provided a source of happiness for him. It also gave us an opportunity to enter into interesting dialogues to include words of affirmation and pride in his accomplishments.

My parents were married for 35 years. Looking back I will say that they really didn't know how to express their love for one another. Some of this was due to the era in which they lived. Outward displays of affection, even within the home, were not encouraged. Despite their shared unresolved heartaches from perceived rejection during childhood, what drew them to each other was the innate need to be loved and a desire to love. This could only have come from the truth of having been made in the image and likeness of God.

I have no information regarding my Dad's Spiritual/Religious upbringing. My Mom was raised in a very liturgical church environment which translated into a highly regimented, law driven, performance based religion. She gave testimony of seeking a relationship with God for many years. Somewhere in her travels, she became acquainted with the Gideons International. This is an organization established in 1899 and is still active today. Anyone who has ever stayed in a Hotel room will find a Bible in the bedside drawer placed there by the Gideons. The following is an excerpt from her autobiography.

"Ever since I was 12, having heard a testimony given by a "Gideon," I prayed almost daily, 'please forgive me for my wrong doings and help me to be what you would have me to be.' I had no understanding of who Jesus was but at about age 15 I started looking for answers. After we moved to Norwood (Massachusetts), I had to go to work. Of 5 potential job offers, the one I wanted least was the one that fit our schedule best. My supervisor answered my questions and led me to a saving knowledge of Jesus Christ. On April 2, 1957, sitting at my desk in a large office, I bowed my head and asked Jesus to come into my life, forgive my sins, and take control of my life. When I looked up, I could see outside that it was raining and the sun was out. I knew that somewhere there was a rainbow and was reminded of one of the few Bible verses I knew, Genesis 9:13, and I knew that God had heard me. "I went home and was determined not to tell your Daddy but to let him see the difference in my life, but I immediately started sharing with you girls and you very quickly prayed to ask Jesus into your lives. I didn't write it down as I felt you were probably only doing it because I said it was the thing to do, but your lives have proven that it was very real at your level of understanding."

❧ ❧

I was 6 years old when Mom made her decision to "follow Jesus." Throughout our lives, she made sure her girls went to church every Sunday morning, Sunday evening, Wednesday evening prayer meeting, and to any other event affording her girls the opportunity to learn more about Jesus. These were impressionable years and definitely gave me a foundation in Biblical training. Daddy did not participate in my Mom's new found faith in God, but never interfered in her involvement and our participation. He had an unspoken, "private" relationship with Jesus, which definitely included his commitment to protect his 5 girls. When my twin and I started dating, he literally had a baseball bat under his bed for any young man who would even dare to hurt his girls. Would he have used it? His bark was definitely worse than his bite but we sure thought it was a good possibility! Mom held our feet to the fire as well when it came to dating. Late home arrivals were not acceptable and we were questioned about everything upon our return.

Another impactful memory as a teenager was the fact that at some point our parents no longer slept in the same bedroom. We were living in a two bedroom home at the time. Mom slept in one of 3 bunk beds set up for my 4 sisters and I in the back bedroom. Daddy took the other bedroom. The reason for this arrangement was not due to any "falling out" or argument. To this day the explanation as to why is still unclear in my mind. All I know is, even though it became the norm experientially, my mind and heart told me otherwise.

Throughout my adult years my precious Mom, with tears in her eyes, would verbalize and apologize for her perceived failures to do and be everything God wanted her to do and be, especially when it came to raising us. Being a mother of 6 myself, I could relate to and enter into her perception. I knew no other. We had both been raised in a behaviorally driven gospel, always fearful of failing God and disappointing Him. We embraced each other, trusting in God's love and forgiveness yet with ongoing regrets and guilt.

Mom was dedicated and disciplined in her desire to grow spiritually. I have sweet childhood memories of her rising early, having quiet time with Jesus. Her Bible, Daily Bread booklet, and Halley's Handbook, were open on the dining room table and her head bowed in prayer. She hardly ever missed a morning. She loved God with all of her heart, mind and soul, and only wanted to obey Him and teach us girls to do the same. In my Mom's later years I treasured our times together, sharing Scripture and songs which spoke to our hearts. To this very day my 4 sisters and I "Rise up and call her Blessed" (*Read Proverbs 31 any translation*).

Mom was not able to experience the joy of having my Daddy on the same Spiritual plane of understanding. Very few times would he attend

> *The implied commission was to be obedient to God, no matter the cost.*

church with us. The motive for such occasions was that his girls were on the platform performing. He was proud of his 5 girls. My Twin and our sister 2 years younger became known as "The Sunbeam Trio." We traveled to many Evangelical Churches in the New England States, singing 3 part harmony, accompanying ourselves on the Ukulele. I will always treasure one Sunday evening service in our Baptist Church, when our Daddy actually sang with my two sisters and I in front of a small but faithful congregation. We sang the old Sunday School song by Stewart Hamblen, "Open Up Your Heart and Let the Sunshine In." He accompanied us on the Ukulele. I know this meant the world to my Mom. She proudly sat in a pew, near the front, where she and her 5 girls would always be found when the church doors were open. Daddy did not give verbal testimony to knowing Jesus relationally until just a few short years prior to his leaving this earth and being in Jesus arms of Love. Mom shared that he had made a "public profession of faith" in a local church down the street from where we had lived. I know beyond a shadow of a doubt that God understood and loved him unconditionally. He was God's beloved child long before my Daddy recognized it.

I'm certain that my precious Mom and Daddy received an extra LONG, BEAR HUG EMBRACE from Jesus upon stepping onto the peaceful shores of Heaven from the turbulent waves of earthly oceans. Daddy died November 24, 1985. Mom died February 22, 2014.

⋅⊙❦⊙⋅

And now my perceptions of my first husband's childhood. I am NOT trying to speak for or on his behalf. I am speaking relative truth based on information gathered over 20 years of marriage. Facts are combined with perspectives and conjectures. Wounds in our childhood can result in ongoing generational brokenness.

He was a Pastor's kid, a Christian School's principal kid, and a missionary's kid, all at the same time. That could only translate into what I will call "a school of hard knocks". His Mom was a quiet, behind the scenes, never wanting to be in the forefront of anything, kind of gal. She was very driven by the fear of what others were thinking of her. In addition to her being a busy Mom to 3 children she had many other roles to play. She served as a Pastor's wife, a teacher's wife, and a Christian School principal's wife. She served in Africa as a Missionary alongside her husband for 35 years with SIM (Sudan Interior Missions). Her "resume" above speaks for itself as to her many responsibilities. This came with enormous burdens to carry.

At the age of 4 and his two sisters a few years older, they were sent off to boarding school many miles away from the compound where they lived. He didn't talk about it much. His 2 older sisters shared with me how he would sob and hang on to his Mother's dress as she, through tears, had to pull him away with a broken heart. She knew that her only precious son, and 2 sweet daughters would perceive this as her separating from and rejecting them. She could not do anything about this. This was the practice of Mission boards in that era. It was God first, Family second. Husbands were driven to preach and teach and work, often exhausted from the demanding long hours. Wives were taught to be submissive and sacrificial in all areas in order to accommodate their husband and the ministry. In my opinion, *the implied commission was to be obedient to God, no matter the cost, resulting in emotional wounding and confusion about the love of God.* In my husband's words, I quote from his book, *From Covered Wagon to Eighteen Wheeler.*

"To this day, I'm not sure who bore the greatest burden . . . the child . . . the parents . . . or the dorm parents. I know I was horribly distraught at leaving my parents for 6 months to go to a boarding school in Africa. That my Mom couldn't see her kids every day, being 500 miles away, about killed her."

Will we be driven by preconceived perceptions arising out of our wound-edness and brokenness?, or will I believe what God believes to be true?

"The foundation of what God believes about you stands immovable and beyond dispute regardless of human opinion or contradiction. The inscription and impression made by the signet ring of God is His signature in your innermost being; He knows you as His own. Let everyone see themselves defined by the name of Christ and depart from everything which does not reveal likeness." 2 Timothy 2:19. (Mirror Study Bible)

This mindset is what my heart embraces and endorses today. In Chapters 9 and 10 I share how God brought me from the bondage of brokenness and woundedness to a place of freedom and healing. Wherever you are in this journey called LIFE, when faced with Words and behaviors contradicting God's character of love, CHOOSE God's Words of absolute truth.

**GOD'S LOVE IS
EVERLASTINGLY UNCONDITIONAL.**

MY STORY

Most stories are a compilation of a person's experiences and events with behavioral reactions and responses to those events. Libraries are filled with Autobiographies and Biographies of both ordinary and extraordinary stories. ALL stories begin with some life form. My physical life on earth began at conception in 1950. My twin made her entrance first and I followed 3 minutes later. BUT . . . my origin of life began in the mind and heart of God long before my birth. God's original blueprint for me, and all of mankind, was and always will be a reflection of Himself. Allow me to quote Francois duToit as he so beautifully translates Psalm 23:2.

> *"By the waters of reflection,*
> *my soul remembers who I am.*
> *He leads me in the footprints of righteousness."*

As my life unfolded it became intertwined with the stories of so many others, all with the same blueprint. When I look back, there were times my true identity was challenged but never invalidated.

Being raised in a Christian home, I was dutifully taught the scriptures by teachers in Fundamental Evangelical churches from the age of 6. I was encouraged to pray, have daily devotions, memorize scripture, and quickly confess and repent of any sins in my daily routine. All of this was for my "spiritual growth", but more importantly "to please God" and maintain "fellowship" with Him. I remember bedtime to be much like the Waltons with a religious spin on it. "Good night Carol, please forgive me." "Good night Susan, please forgive me." "Goodnight Anita, please forgive me." . . . Goodnight Wendy, please forgive me." I'm serious! Nothing wrong with "keeping short accounts," and "not letting the sun go down upon your wrath," but for me there was a subconscious fear associated with this nightly practice. Obedience meant approval. Disobedience meant disapproval. That is why I never went to bed without asking God to forgive me for anything I had done to displease Him.

God did not feel as close to me as Jesus. I knew He was mostly written about in the Old Testament. I also knew he had given the 10 Commandments which I memorized early in childhood. I was taught that these were an important list of behaviors to obey and that it would please Him to do so. To tell you the truth, the Old Testament was filled with stories where God became very angry if His laws were disobeyed.

The **Holy Spirit** was somewhat of an enigma to me as a child. I definitely did not have a relationship with him. I don't really remember understanding who or what He was. Later in life I was taught that God was going to send the Spirit to us after Jesus left earth and went back up to Heaven with God. When I "asked Jesus into my heart" at some level of understanding I was told that His Spirit now lived in me because of my prayer to invite Jesus in. When I grew older, I also remember the Holy Spirit being associated with the well known "charismatic

> *I remember bedtime to be much like the Waltons with a religious spin on it.*

movement" introduced in 1958. Most fundamental Christians did not fully embrace this sect. Sadly, this brought confusion and

> *Manmade conditions fanned the flames of fear and self righteousness.*

division among believers. I remember that we were not encouraged to attend these churches because of the beliefs and practices found within their teachings.

One thing was certain. I knew **Jesus** loved me and died for my sins and That was enough. As a little girl I made my life's verse Philippians 1:21 from the KJV. "For me to live is Christ, and to die is gain." I was "sold out to Jesus". I really tried to please Him by being obedient to my parents, and I was taught to ask for forgiveness when I knew I had not been "a good girl".

I wanted to be perfectly obedient with the reality of knowing I wasn't. Unfortunately this mindset carried a very unintentional arrogance or self righteousness. I was often perceived as, well . . . a "miss goody two shoes". According to the dictionary, the definition of a "goody two shoes" is

> *"a person who always does everything right*
> *and always follows the rules,*
> *so much so that it becomes annoying."*

I'm talking about a lot of annoyance from the age of 6 to 60+. I had developed a set of beliefs which fostered detrimental mindsets. Man made conditions fanned the flames of fear and self righteousness.

At the time I did not know that I was living in "sin consciousness", rather than being conscious of sin. There is a distinct difference. The former is driven by fear. The latter is driven by Love. Living out of the truth of our identity and awareness of God's unconditional love, is a platform on which to evaluate behavior and its consequences as God sees it. Asking for forgiveness becomes a love driven response, as we agree with God and respond appropriately without guilt and shame and fear of rejection.

⋅⋅◌𝕰 𝕲◌⋅⋅

I graduated from Senior High School in 1968, in Norwood, Massachusetts. A week after I graduated, our family moved to Santa Cruz, California. In 1969 my twin and I enrolled in Cabrillo College in Aptos. In 1971 we were in the first graduating class to receive an Associate of Science Degree in Nursing. My childhood dream of becoming a nurse was coming true.

Soon thereafter I passed my state board and became a bona-fide Registered Nurse.

> *In this "intertwining" of lives, I had to believe God was orchestrating something in my life.*

Going to Bible School was always a goal of my twin and mine when finishing High School. My parents did not have the means to assist us in this venture. Subsequently we worked one year in our local hospital, as licensed RNs, to earn our tuition to attend Multnomah School of the Bible (MSB) in Portland, Oregon. They offered a one year graduate program of intensive Bible Training for students with professional degrees. We graduated in 1973 with a Certificate in Bible. (This School is now known as Multnomah University.) "Missions" was a huge focus within the Bible training at MSB. I had a passion welling up within me to go to Africa as a Missionary Nurse.

It was also understood that an "Mrs. degree" was always a possible option. There was a standing riddle at MSB. "What do a rooster, a Yankee, and a Multnomah girl have in common? The answer: "A rooster goes, cock-a-doodle-doo, a yankee goes, yankee doodle doo, and a Multnomah girl goes, any dude'll do." I was an exception to that rule. As much as I

94

dreamed of being married and having children, I was scared to death of any guy who wanted a relationship with me. I surmised this was partially due to not having had brothers or male cousins to interact with, coupled with a very protective and somewhat sheltered upbringing. I did like to have the attention of boys but developed a quick recoil reaction to any pursuit. That being said, there was a young man in his 3rd and final year at MSB who made his intentions known to me. I remember a conversation we had shortly before graduation in which he expressed his strong convictions that "I was the one" and he believed we would be married by the following year. I could not dismiss this. In my mind God was possibly revealing His will to me.

After graduation in June of 1973, I was faced with a very important and difficult decision. During those post graduate months I resumed working as a Nurse in the Santa Cruz area. I made a decision to take the necessary steps to become a foreign Missionary Nurse. I applied to Sudan Interior Missions. Meanwhile, this patient and hopeful young man traveled the distance from Grants Pass, Oregon to Santa Cruz California on weekends. We had mutually agreed upon a continued relationship even if long distance. He was living with friends while his parents were serving as Missionaries in Sudan. He had been raised in Africa until his teen years. In this "intertwining" of lives, I had to believe God was orchestrating something in my life.

My Mom was always reminding us girls that "the Lord can't guide an anchored ship." I was torn between the two options my mind and Heart were contemplating. Do I choose Africa or this relationship? I definitely didn't want to get this wrong in the eyes of God. Did I have feelings for this man? Yes . . . but definitely suppressed. Because of my insecurities, my fear of "missing God's will" mindset had to catch up with my heart's knowing that I could trust God in this relationship during those several months. It went without saying that I prayed fervently for an answer. I asked the Lord to open and close doors so I would know. I felt the answer actually came when I was turned down by the one and only

Mission Board I had applied to. I took this as a "closed door" and an invitation to go "full speed ahead" into this budding relationship.

One year later, just as he had predicted, I married this Multnomah dude on June 29th, 1974. His patient persistence captured my heart. I will never forget my wedding day. I could not have been more certain that this was God's will. He was my soulmate. God met me where I was in my mind and heart. He removed any doubts and fears. Only God can do that. We made our residence in Grants Pass, Oregon, moving into a home he had newly constructed.

As a side note, my husband's roommate at MSB married my "womb mate". Yes, my identical twin. My husband tells the story of having seen my twin and I singing together in a chapel service at MSB. He told his roommate about us and basically said one was spoken for, but he could have the other one. My twin and his roommate actually beat us to the "altar" by 6 months. They had 3 children . . . each being born 6 months ahead of our first 3. My husband and I went on to have 3 more.

In 1975 our first little girl was born. I had prayed for a little girl with long hair who could sing. God saw fit to answer that prayer. Every 15 to 21 months thereafter God blessed us with 5 more amazingly gifted kids. 6 kids in 8 years . . . 4 girls and 2 boys in that order. Our family became known as the "Von Nash Family Singers", harmonizing together like the well known Austrian Von Trapp Family portrayed in "The Sound of Music". Little did I know that there would be another similarity in the years to come. Our family would face the treacherous journey over proverbial Mountains which would seem insurmountable.

My husband and I, and our precious children were involved in "church planting" from 1975 to around 1988. This is a term used when being sent to a designated location within the U.S. and establishing a viable church. We were blessed to start churches in both Washington State, and Montana.

We were considered "Home Missionaries" under an organization known as N.I.C.E. (Northwest Independent Church Extension). This was a branch of the IFCA (Independent Fundamental Churches of America). We were required to raise our own financial support before and often during our endeavors. We had many faithful monthly supporters, but as some of you may understand, this income would fluctuate from month to month. My husband put in many long hours, working in many different capacities made available to him. He was a rancher, construction worker, farmer, and pastor/teacher. He worked hard and instilled a good work ethic in our children. As a family we were blessed to live in two homes he built from the ground up while in the ministry. He also built a beautiful church building for our little congregation in Augusta, Montana. He designed a hitching post out front for cowboys to tie up their horses while attending church. In 1989 we left Montana and moved back to beautiful Southern Oregon.

We experienced the typical "bumps and bruises" common in most marriages. The years of raising 6 little ones, and juggling ministry, took its toll on both of us. I poured my heart into my children while my husband poured his heart into ministry and work. This is a recipe for communication breakdown within any relationship if one is not careful to guard against it. Because the "D" word (divorce) was never an option for us while dating and considering marriage, I knew we could and would get through this season.

During a time when I sensed my Husband to be discouraged and in "burn out" mode, I held a dinner in his honor. Being a Pastor can be taxing and exhausting at times. There is a lot of giving of yourself required which includes hours of listening to and counseling those with heartaches and challenges within relationships. Sad to say there are many marriages that "don't make it in the ministry" because of it.

> *The years of raising 6 little ones, and juggling ministry, took its toll on both of us.*

I contacted key people from all of our previous church families to come and join in a celebration to encourage and honor him. People came from Montana and Washington to share how God had used my husband's teaching to make a difference in their life. Little did I know, he was fighting restlessness in our marriage. I was either naive or blind to any warning signs. Not long after this celebratory event, and then 20 years of marriage, my husband's restlessness gave birth to what I feared the most. I was not enough. Our marriage and ministry was soon to come to an end.

That was the beginning of a long and unexpected journey.

My husband was counseling a young woman who attended a Bible Study we held in our home for young married couples. Despite the wise counsel from his Dad to "always keep a desk between you and a crying woman", He fell victim to her tears and subsequently assisted her in leaving her husband. He provided housing for her, and soon moved in. It was not long after when He said the heart wrenching words to me, "I don't love you any more."

My husband's restlessness gave birth to what I feared the most. I was not enough.

I will never forget the day I was served with divorce papers by a close friend of my husband who was also a Deacon in our church. During the ensuing months and years I had held on to my commitment to our marriage while praying for his return. My "so-journey with words" was daunting. My heart and mind were in constant battle. I attempted, in my pain, to rightly divide words of truth from lies on both a horizontal and vertical level. I clung to my Bible, holding onto every shred of hope found in the words of Scripture. I felt lost, unloved, and unlovely. I had lost my identity. Even though my husband willingly stepped down from his position as pastor, I still considered myself in a role as "Pastor's wife" to our congregation. Knowing the church would be calling another

Pastor, I chose to leave our church in order for the next couple to be fully embraced. I started attending various churches in the area, always met with love and the utmost support.

In the ensuing 3- 5 years I enjoyed planning my 3 oldest daughter's weddings a year apart, and raising 3 still at home, all while working full time as an RN in our local Urgent Care. Within those years I had entrenched myself in a group called "Covenant Keepers". They believed in the healing of broken marriages. They taught I was not free to remarry because my "husband" was still alive. Even though divorced, I was to stand firm, immovable in my commitment and vows. I was to trust God to bring him back to me. They also taught me that I was to take him back with no questions asked, no matter the behavior. Because of my upbringing I was somehow good with that. God and I were partnering to become a statistic of reconciliation rather than one of failure.

I will never forget the day I looked out my front door and saw my Husband pacing the sidewalk in front of my home. He had been married for a relatively short period of time to the woman he left me for. He was now facing the heartache of his relatively new bride divorcing him for an acquaintance of his. I remember my heartfelt compassion for him. I was also rejoicing inside and pinching myself. Could this be real? Has God answered my prayer for the healing of my marriage? Was He giving me a second chance to DO BETTER and RIGHT THE WRONGS causing my husband to leave our marriage?

Not too many weeks had passed before we renewed our vows and signed a second marriage certificate. Our 6 precious children took part in the ceremony that day. Our family of 8 sang my song of testimony by Steve Green, "We are a Household of Faith". This was truly surreal. In the years following our divorce, my husband had added long haul Trucking to his resume. On this our second wedding day His spit shined 18 wheeler was proudly parked outside the little country church. This was our means of transportation for a honeymoon to Montana. My husband had left

God and I were partnering to become a statistic of reconciliation rather than one of failure.

his heart in that BIG SKY Country and wanted us to relocate there. A few weeks prior to our wedding I surprised my husband by obtaining my CDL permit in order to be a "trucker mama" by his side. I planned on getting some valuable practice over the hundreds of miles ahead, and subsequently planned on getting my CDL License upon our return home. I had always prided myself in the fact that I could back up a U-Haul trailer with no coaching. Not so much with an 18 wheeler flatbed trailer. I also never could get the hang of shifting without using the clutch. This is a trick truckers use to save wear and tear on the gears. I assure you I caused more wear and tear with all the grinding attempts to get it right than he ever saved. One thing for sure . . . I have a lot more respect for truckers having had this unforgettable experience.

Upon returning home, the plan was for me to continue working as a nurse for a while longer, while my husband returned to the I-5 corridor. He would return home in June for our youngest son's graduation from High school and we would then discuss our future plans. In the meanwhile we stayed in touch by phone. Often I would stand outside and look at the moon, knowing he was looking at the same moon 100's of miles away. My heart rejoiced in having my husband return to me. As June was approaching, I remember a few phone conversations in which I sensed in him an emotional withdrawal from me. I prayed it was nothing, but still being in a somewhat vulnerable place of healing from rejection, I couldn't dismiss the fear and doubts. Not wanting to even believe such thoughts, I went into denial and was unable to discuss my feelings with him or anyone else.

Graduation week arrived. We sat on the outdoor bleachers of the Grants Pass High School Football field that warm summer evening, proud of our son's accomplishment. But my mind was distracted. My heart was confirming the distance I had sensed in our previous phone conversations. He was quiet, and somewhat aloof. I am unclear as to the timing of this next event. He was to head back to the I-5 corridor sometime that week. One thing is crystal clear. I was not prepared for the note found on my kitchen counter the day of his departure. As gently as he could, he wrote that he did not love me and had only come back for the sake of our kids. He expressed that he knew he was hurting me again, and was very sorry.

From the very beginning, our children could not fully embrace his coming back. Those who were married at the time, along with their spouses, cautioned my "taking him back too soon". Despite their feelings, they wanted to believe it was for real, and shared in my joy of their Dad's return and seemingly repentant heart.

It was difficult to share the note with my children. It only served to confirm their original lack of trust. Their hopes and dreams were extinguished while rekindling the flames of resentment and anger. I was living with the reality of 6 wounded and Broken hearted children who felt rejected. This was the greatest burden to bear at the time. What was somewhat unexpected was the peace that came over me when reading the note. My mind and heart were telling me that I had "DONE" everything I could to "RIGHT my BEHAVIOR" during this second chance. It seemed that God was bringing closure to this relationship. There were still times when I would experience feelings of guilt and shame over a failed marriage mixed with fears of disappointing God. He was so patient with me when I allowed the tentacles of man driven laws to bind me up in my mind. *In my heart I knew God had placed me under the protective shadow of His wings even when I felt like I was walking through the valley of "the shadow death." (Psalm 23 any translation)*

I continued working in Urgent Care. (By the way . . . I never pursued my Truckers license.) Life was a mixture of joys and sorrows. Our remaining 3 children were married not long thereafter, and Grandchildren were soon to come. Each one of our children developed a relationship with their Dad individually in their own ways and in their own time. I have to admit that my legalistic approach toward my husband had fostered an unwillingness to have a relationship with him. My justification and rationalization for my rejecting/shunning him was based on how I interpreted the Scriptures (or more correctly, how others interpreted them for me.) If you think you are doing the right thing (even if it is based on a doctrinal belief), and it is contradicting God's character of unconditional love, it is clearly the wrong thing. My identity was wrapped up in a legalistic and performance driven mindset. I look back over this chapter in my life and marvel at how God met me with Grace and Mercy as he did my husband. God knew where we were emotionally, physically and spiritually.

I am writing this book to give testimony to the fact that God will enter into ALL choices and consequences, good or bad, with no condemnation or rejection. This includes the consequences we experience when found within the "crossfire" of other's choices.

From motorcycle tragedies to broken relationships in 3 out of 6 of our children's marriages, God entered into our brokenness and woundedness. ALL involved in my story were on their own personal journey. I can only speak for myself in what I am about to write. Looking back I believe with all my heart that I did not fully and freely understand God's love. I was lost in a quagmire of doctrines emphasizing my DOing the right thing rather than the absolute truth of BEing who God knows me to be. The question Jesus asked "Who do you say that I AM" must be answered. When we understand who He is, we will understand who we are. When looking at the Scriptures, do we see Jesus? When we look at Jesus, do we see our innocence? Our believing this does not make it so. Our belief awakens us to the reality that His identity is my identity. (John 14:20 any translation) Jesus said,

> "... *I am in my Father, you are in me and I am in you.*"

When looking back over my story, I feel compassion for my husband and myself, and gratitude to God. That may seem odd to you, but it is true.

I can only speak for myself. Interpretation of scripture played a huge role in my reactions and responses.

There is no "if only" from God's perspective . . . only I Am!

I behaved in ways familiar to my doctrinal beliefs. In my opinion, my husbands and my upbringing under the performance driven law of works, undermined our marriage. Doctrines of men contradicted the absolute truth of our identity. If only we had seen ourselves cradled in God's unconditional love, void of expectations and condemnations. If only we had known ourselves as we were truly known by God. *(see 1 Corinthians 13 and John 17)* I do find comfort in knowing that there is no "if only" from God's perspective . . . only I Am!

I cannot control other people's beliefs and behaviors which may cause heartache and pain for all involved. I can only choose to live in the absolute truth of my identity, what God believes to be true about me. In this mindset I can experience peace in the midst of woundedness and brokenness from choices I make or those made by others. What words are motivating you to continue believing what you believe? Are they words of LIFE or DEATH?

"Intertwining with God's thoughts concerning you,
immediately causes you to escape the weariness
of the do it yourself times and
mount up with wings like an eagle,
to run and not be weary,
to walk and not faint!"
(Isaiah 40:31 Mirror Study Bible)

"When you pass through the waters,
I will be with you;
and when you pass through the rivers,
they will not sweep over you.
When you walk through the fire
you will not be burned;
the flames will not set you ablaze."
(Isaiah 43:2 NIV)

BREAKING FREE

"Every Love Story is beautiful,
but ours is my favorite."

For 10 years I continued to pray, "God, if two can't be better than one, then I'll stay one." I knew He knew the desire of my heart was to remarry, but my involvement in "Covenant Keepers" always caused unrest in my heart and mind. I had had a couple of casual relationships that went nowhere. This was by God's design for sure. My ongoing unrest and downright confusion doctrinally, prevented me from "pushing the envelope". Was I free to remarry or not? There were theologians on both sides of the fence on this issue.

I had recently moved into the outskirts of town and wanted to get plugged into a local Church. Spirit led me to an Evangelical Church where I became involved in a home group. Interestingly the group's name was, "The wild bunch". Being a very fundamental, black or white, right or wrong type of gal, I was sure I could "minister" to them and "guide them into all truth". Little did I know how much these treasured people would minister to me. Many of them were from the Gospel Rescue Mission located just a few blocks away from where we gathered each week. They would come and go like a revolving door. Often old or lingering strongholds with Alcohol and Drugs would pull them away.

One evening, a new fellow showed up. I was drawn to his somewhat toothless smile. He had an open Bible in front of him, ready and eager to learn. His name was Lloyd. He was asked to share his testimony of recovery from a 30+ year addiction to Methamphetamines. The resolve in his heart to follow Christ was confirmed in his words and revealed in his demeanor. I was disappointed when he did not return the following week. Occasionally I would see him from a distance during greeting times at church. This alleviated my fear that he may have become a statistic of one returning to old lifestyles. Lloyd did not know I was watching him from afar. His sweet manner with people and his infectious smile continued to tug at my heart.

Now, let me provide some relevant background information. Within the 10 years following my divorce, I had continued working as an RN, at that time in Urgent Care. I became quite proficient in the procedure of ear wax removal. After many years of performing this procedure in a clinical setting, I had started my own business, DBA "Ears to Hear" in 2005. I introduced myself to the Hearing Aide proprietors in the Rogue Valley. Year to date I have and continue to serve well over 1500 patients. The smiles and sheer delight from the elderly who thought they were deaf and could suddenly hear again, is my reward. "He who has ears to hear, let him hear." These were Jesus' words recorded in Matthew 11:15. In meeting physical needs, God gave me many opportunities to minister to my patients emotionally and Spiritually as well.

One day I dropped by to see the owner of a local hearing aid company, to give him a report on one of his patient referrals. Who should come out from the back office to the front desk but Lloyd. He had a white lab jacket on and perfectly combed silver hair. This time, he had a full set of pearly whites, having obtained dentures since I had seen him several weeks before. Wow! He looked like a million bucks! My heart skipped a beat . . . ok, maybe 2 or 3. Unbeknownst to me, the owner of this Hearing Aid business was Lloyd's Uncle.

He was being trained in this industry and was placed in charge while his Uncle was on vacation. I would soon find out that Lloyd was also being spiritually mentored by him.

He greeted me with his beautiful smile and professional demeanor. I reciprocated in a like manner, while trying to remain composed. He then asked, "Do I know you from somewhere?" I told him that It could have been when he shared his personal testimony at "the wild bunch" Bible Study I attended. I also told him that I frequently sang on the worship team in church. Lloyd seemed to remember the Bible Study event but at that time he didn't know me from Adam, let alone Eve. In all reality he had paid no particular attention to me except as one in the group. I then proceeded to take care of the business at hand which had brought me into the office in the first place. I left with a huge smile on my face. You see, I had told the Lord that I would not pursue any man. He would have to "bring him to me". As a side note . . . not long before this, my second daughter had asked me if I ever thought I would remarry. It had been 8 years since her Dad left the second time. My response was, "Yes." I then followed that affirmation with this statement. "There is this guy I met at Bible study, and if he ever came into my life and asked me out, I would go." Do you think I remembered this conversation with my daughter when I was standing face to face with Lloyd? That's a no brainer!

After I did my running of errands, I checked my cell phone which I often leave in the car while tending to my patients. There was a text message notification. I remember saying to myself, "I hope that's Lloyd." I wish I had saved that message. It went something like this. "Hi, this is Lloyd. I really like you, and would love to get to know you. Would you like to go out sometime?" I think my heart beat drowned out the rest of

This began a Love Story that only God could have written.

that message. He must have asked me to call him back . . . which I promptly did . . . as if I needed an invitation at that point. Lloyd told me later that while he was leaving that message, he "was on cloud 15, dancing around the store." To this day he remembers the long plaid dress I wore into the office that day, which still hangs in my closet. (smile)

This began a Love Story that only God could have written. We went out a few times and attended that same home group together. It became very clear to both of us that we were being drawn to each other and for all the right reasons. But, my story would be incomplete without sharing Lloyd's testimony.

His early childhood did not include church attendance. After his Dad was introduced to Christianity, now looking back, Lloyd describes his upbringing as being fundamental, evangelical, and performance driven. In a nutshell he remembers that "everything changed". In the BC days (before Christianity), when Lloyd was 4 years old, his Dad introduced him to the world of racing quarter midgets. It became his first love. "I lived to race, and raced to live." In fact he won his first trophy at the age of 4. When Lloyd was 9, and Christianity had become the new normal, a very significant event happened. With no communication or explanation, Lloyd's Dad sold all race cars and equipment. Race days were always held on Saturdays and Sundays. His Dad believed it was not "Godly" to put racing ahead of going to church. He soon moved his family from California to Oregon. Lloyd did not understand why his Dad and his new life took away something so important to him. What's worse, he was never allowed to question why. Not long after, their family moved from Oregon to Canada where his Dad attended Prairie Bible Institute. He became an ordained minister and felt the call to take his family to Ireland to serve as Missionaries.

When Lloyd was 17, he wanted to return stateside. His Dad supported him on this but with a strong desire that he attend Bible School. Lloyd agreed that he would, and even looked forward to doing so. He honored this commitment and was accepted into Sacramento Bible College in California.

Within his first year, he and some friends attended a pool hall for sheer recreational pleasure. Word of this activity leaked out to the School's Dean of men which resulted in Lloyd and his buddies being placed on probation. Here was his reaction in his own words.

"I'm done with this. I've been sheltered from the world all my life. I want to see what the world is all about!"

He continued to make choices contrary to his Christian upbringing. His life soon resembled that of the Prodigal son's. He developed a serious addiction to Methamphetamines as well as becoming involved in unhealthy relationships. For many years he was a functional addict. He would have seasons of being clean. He established a very successful business in the Rogue Valley, grossing close to a million dollars a year. His victories were soon swallowed up in his addictive behavior and relationships. He suffered the consequences of 3 failed marriages and lost everything. This included his successful business and active involvement with his 3 children. The paranoia which ensued with ongoing drug abuse became insurmountable at times.

In his earlier adult years his Uncle, aware of his lifestyle choices, reached out to him. He saw Lloyd as a "lost sheep" so to speak, who needed to be "brought back into the fold". Lloyd knew he was "not done run'n and gun'n", and could not, nor would he ever take advantage of his Uncle. He also did not want to burn a potential bridge for later. After having lost everything, he finally accepted his

His life soon resembled that of the Prodigal son's.

God never once gave up on Lloyd, or reneged on His promises.

Uncle's invitation for help. He had reached what many know to be, "rock bottom". He was given a little Shack in the woods on his Uncle's property. It was here he began listening to the Bible and gospel music on cassette tapes. He would sing at the top of his lungs, *I can only imagine* and, *Here I am to worship*, along with many others. To this day Lloyd can be heard singing the refrain, "I'll never know how much it cost to see my sins upon that cross." Truly God was continuing the good work He had started in his life before the foundation of the world. God never once gave up on Lloyd, or reneged on His promises.

This brings us back to where I left off in my unexpected encounter with Lloyd that day. His apprenticeship was well underway within his Uncles Hearing Aid Business. His Spiritual growth was evidenced in his willingness to humble himself under his Uncle's non-negotiable disciplines to help Lloyd get to where he so desperately wanted and needed to be. Allowing his Uncle to manage his finances was key to his recovery. He gives testimony to the fact that this piece of accountability was imperative to form new habits where old ones had taken over. As a result bills were paid, money saved, and necessities taken care of. Thus the pearly whites (false teeth) to replace that toothless smile I fell in love with.

I had met Lloyd when he was 18 months clean from his 30+ year addiction. When my family and friends became aware of my budding relationship in this context . . . well, let's just say their concerns, spoken or unspoken, left very little to my imagination as to what they were thinking. For them his past became the elephant in the room, let alone a HUGE RED FLAG. The one question frequently asked by family and friends was, "How do you know he won't go back to his drug use?" If these words were not spoken, they were definitely implied by their reservations to enter into my joy. Both Lloyd and I knew that their reactive concerns

110

were coming from a sincere love for me. We also knew that time was needed in order to establish a trustworthy relationship and satisfy their unspoken and understandable requirement for accountability in Lloyd's life. We made a heartfelt commitment to be other centered and wait a substantial amount of time before "tying the knot". We never regretted this decision. We were able to demonstrate our love and commitment to each other while showing respect and honor to those who loved us and only wanted the best for us. It was a win-win choice. My husband still tells our story to include having a proverbial piece of plexiglas in his back pocket to pull out when our lips started to head toward each other.

As far as my response to their question, "How do you know he won't go back to drugs?," the following became my predictable repy.

"I was married 20 years to a man who
I met in Bible School, was a pastor for 20 years,
Established 2 churches and a Christian School,
a son of a Missionary/Pastor,
and who left me for a woman 20 years younger than me."

Though coming from a familiar performance driven mindset at the time, I believe this was the beginning of God reinforcing a Spirit driven instinctive belief in me that behavior does not determine our identity. My response was not meant to condemn and should not be read with condemnation. My Faith then, and now, was and is in Christ, and Christ alone.

⁘

Back to where I left off. I was stopped in my tracks a couple of months into our courtship. Doubts crept into my mind as to the validity of our relationship as far as God was concerned. These doubts had nothing to do with his past, or my love for him. I never once feared he would go back to his former lifestyle. I was struggling with a mindset having been established within indoctrination for 50+ years.

"Am I really free to remarry, Lord?"

This was my prayer. I had to know. What is so surreal is the indisputable fact that God knew I needed to get this settled in my mind once and for all. I believe now, with all my heart, God wanted me to know His heart in this matter of divorce and remarriage even more than I did. He saw ALL of what He had in store for me with this man.

I had to tell Lloyd that I could not go on in our relationship until I settled this issue in my mind and heart. It was not fair to him to do so. His response made it even harder for me to put the relationship on hold. He did not "hold on to my ankles" nor cry, "How can you do this to me, to us? You know I'm the one for you and you for me." Sad to say, the simple fact was this. If he had said these words, indicative of codependency (a common pattern of behavior in those suffering from addiction) I would have probably taken that as my answer to NOT continue the relationship. Instead, his response was, "I will wait for you." He did not try to contact me. Rather, he stepped aside with quiet resolve and an unwavering trust in God. He waited while showing preference and honor to me. He was ever so present in my heart and mind. I knew he was praying for me . . . for us.

One day in desperation I prayed. "God, I'm not hearing your voice. I need to know in a tangible way." God met me where I was in my confused state of mind. When I was faithless, He remained faithful. (2 Timothy 2:13)

As I recall, the phone rang within 10 minutes of that prayer. It was a call from a Missionary friend who was home on furlough and requested his ears be cleaned before returning to the Philippines where he and his wife were serving. Now it was not an audible voice, but as sure as my heart was beating, Spirit gave me the assurance that this was the man I was to talk to regarding my question on the doctrines of divorce and remarriage. I made an appointment for him to come to my home for the procedure. I then asked if I could share with him what was weighing so heavily on my heart. He was more than willing to listen.

> *God wanted me to know His heart in this matter of divorce and remarriage even more than I did.*

This man was a staunch, evangelical, fundamental, Bible teaching, pulpit pounding Missionary. When Spirit had told me to share with him, I prayed this prayer. "Lord, whatever he says, I will do." Through my tears I shared my heartfelt desire to OBEY GOD. As I sat across from him in my living room, his head was down. He showed little to no emotion, or eye contact. During my recitation of thoughts I could tell he was deep in thought and listening to every word. When I finally finished, there were a few seconds of silence which seemed like forever. I was sure he was going to tell me I had to cut the relationship off in order to be obedient to God's Word. He raised his head and looked me square in the eyes. He declared these words with what sounded like all authority from heaven,

"MARRY THE MAN!"

My tears of confusion and doubt turned to joy. I know all of heaven was rejoicing that day. I was experiencing a freedom that can only come from an unconditionally loving God. He knew this girl's heart desire was to OBEY. **His heart's desire was for me to be FREE.**

In our upbringing, obedience was always linked to right behavior in order to please God. I challenge you to look up the word OBEY in its original meaning. I will summarize it in this way. To be obedient is to know and embrace the heart of God. The following verse has become my heart's testimony and declaration to this present day.

"He is your freedom from anything from which the law could never free you! Find your firm footing in this freedom. Do not let religion trip you up again and harness you to a system of rules and obligations."
(Galatians 5:1 Mirror Study Bible)

"And they lived happily ever after." Lloyd and I were married November 6, 2010. There is so much more I could share, but suffice it to say, "And they lived happily ever after."

Lloyd's daily demonstration of God's Unconditional Love toward me, my 6 children, 20 grandchildren and 2 great grandchildren and more to come, has been a healing balm to my soul. Lloyd and I and God are ONE.

"Those who wait on the Lord shall renew their strength; They shall mount up with wings like eagles, they shall run and not be weary, they shall walk and not faint." (Isaiah 40:31 NKJV)

The word "wait" is a figurative translation of the Hebrew word "qavah". The literal translation is "to bind together like a cord or twisting or winding of a strand of cord or rope". This is a good example of how translations often have a choice of meaning for a particular word. Looking at the context is very important in making that choice. "Wait" is the verbiage used in most of the translations of the Bible I own. To me, wait is an action word, a task I must do in order to receive. In this context I must wait in order to get strength, fly, run, and walk. It infers separation from the source with conditions to receive. On the other hand, being entwined, or woven together in a cord represents a place where I am. The strength is already mine by virtue of my inclusion in Him. Therefore there are no conditions for flying, running, and walking. Embracing my identity awakens me to the absolute truth that I AM STRONG, I CAN FLY, I CAN RUN, I CAN WALK WITHOUT FAINTING. Oh the power of words. In this case, the word "wait" was not a mistranslation or an inserted word, but rather a choice made by the translator to use the figurative meaning rather than the literal. From my perspective, in the broader context of Isaiah's writings, the literal meaning is the better translation.

114

*"Intertwining with God's thoughts concerning you, immediately causes you
to escape the weariness of the do it yourself times
and mount up with wings like an eagle, to run and not be weary,
to walk and not faint!"*
(Isaiah 40:31 Mirror Study Bible)

Our love story has been seamless from the beginning. We continue in the realization that our lives are an entanglement of THREE strands which cannot easily be untangled (*Ecclesiastes 4:12*). Lloyd and I have experienced the joy of knowing who God is and who God says we are based on God's character of unconditional love. All of us have a story filled with relative truth unique to us. But, we all share the absolute truth of origin to be in a loving union with God before the world began. This absolute truth is common to all mankind regardless of whether we believe it or not.

Lloyd and I are still asking the questions, "Why do I believe what I believe?" and "Why is it so important to me?" What we have called our "Road to Emmaus" is one on which we will never look back. Both of us are giving an ongoing testimony, as did those disciples walking with Jesus recorded in Luke 24:32 (ESV) *"Did not our hearts burn within us while he talked to us on the road, while He opened to us the Scriptures?"* It is still the Father's heart's desire to "open up to us the Scriptures" and lead us into all truth. HE IS THE WORD.

Our lives are an entanglement of THREE strands which cannot easily be untangled.
(Ecclesiastes 4:12)

We challenge you to apply logical thinking to what you believe. KNOW that you KNOW that you KNOW what you believe about God is lining up with what God believes to be TRUE about YOU! The opposite is to live in fear and rejection, in a lost identity under the law of works.

"Christ defines your faith; He is your freedom from Anything from which the law could never free you. Find your firm footing in this freedom.

Do not let religion trip you up again and harness you to a system of rules and obligations." (Galatians 5:1 Mirror Study Bible)

Your identity defines freedom and freedom defines You!

What an incredible journey we all face every moment of every day. May we continue to sojourn with words with the MIND OF CHRIST. May we never allow ourselves to become complacent, apathetic, or stagnant in our thinking. Nor become so arrogant that we resort to slander and judgment toward those challenging our beliefs. Entrust your beliefs to THE WORD. He will affirm the Truth you know, and challenge your beliefs which are not in alignment with what God believes. Your identity defines freedom and freedom defines You!

God's blueprint for ALL mankind is the parchment upon which His words of Unconditional Love are written with indelible crimson ink.

LOST AND FOUND

Yesterday I took a walk down memory lane while perusing an antique shop in my home town of Grants Pass, OR. I ran across a sign which read,

**"Nothing is truly lost
unless Mom can't find it."**

Even if you aren't a parent, you can relate. In raising 6 children, there were a lot of things that went MIA . . . socks being at the top of the list. I swear the dryer ate them. We literally had a huge garbage bag full of unmatched socks. There were two common responses when a request was made to find any lost items. "It's not mine." or "I can't find it!"

There are 3 Biblical accounts, also referred to as parables, in which Jesus describes something or someone being lost and found. Allow me to place them in context with a statement made in the second chapter of this book.

Something or someone cannot be lost without first belonging. Here are the stats in each of these 3 examples found in Luke chapter 15.

There is **one** lost sheep, **one** lost coin, and **one** lost son (AKA the Prodigal son). I emphasize the word ONE intentionally. The shepherd had 100 sheep *(verse 4)*. The Woman had 10 silver coins *(verse 8)*.

God's motivation to love will always be in the context of intrinsic value.

The Father had 2 sons *(verse 11)*. When you read this passage of scripture, I can assure you that the reaction within the knowledge of that which was lost is significantly different from the reaction my children had toward lost socks. Please bear with me on this. Whether we are dealing with socks, sheep, coins, or children, there will always be a direct correlation between the VALUE placed on, and the MOTIVATION to seek and find, that which is lost. In our English language there are several adjectives which can accompany the word value and describe motivation.

These are worth considering when exploring words in context of God's unconditional love.

Intrinsic

Inherent

Extrinsic

Innate

According to Collins Dictionary, the word **intrinsic** means; *"Belonging to the real nature of the thing; not dependent on external circumstances; essential, inherent."* In every definition given for **extrinsic** it was stated as *the opposite of intrinsic. Value and motivation are driven by external circumstances, in some cases with comparisons and time constraints. It is always associated with desire for a reward or to avoid punishment.* In my opinion, God's motivation to love will always be in the context of intrinsic value. Doctrines of men will always be in a context of Extrinsic value.

Let's look at the word **inherent** in Oxford Languages: *"Existing in someone or something as a permanent, essential quality or attribute."* In each of the 3 parables, an undeniable intrinsic inherent value was ascribed to the sheep, coin, and son. The Shepherd, Woman,

There is a direct correlation between the VALUE placed on, and the MOTIVATION to seek and find, that which is lost.

and Father sought after that which was lost with absolute resolve. The motivation came from within with no concern about time constraints. Nor did they make a comparison to the 99 sheep or the 9 other silver coins. In the story of the Prodigal son, which we will look at in more detail later, it is made clear that the Father placed equal value on both of his sons. Motivation to find came from within.

In keeping with my premise to establish absolute truths regarding God's unconditional love for ALL mankind, another word came to mind. Could I link the word INNATE to the word VALUE? Mirriam-Webster defines **innate** as: *"existing in, belonging to, or determined by factors present in an individual from birth. Belonging to the essential nature of something."* I found this definition to be congruent with my premise, despite the following statement made by Neil Eisenberg, a Psychologist, content writer, blogger, author, and investigative reporter.

"Since the word 'innate' is defined as; originating in or derived from the mind or the constitution of the intellect rather than from experience, 'innate value' cannot be defined in terms of 'value' since we all perceive everything based on our unique value system. Since everybody's value system is different, there is no real innate value to anything."

In my opinion, this contradicts the logic of God and reflects a lost identity. When our value system and subsequent mindset is focused on "my truth", "your truth", "their truth", it will always result in extrinsic value and behaviorally driven motivations. It is my opinion that *In the logic (mind) of God, innate, intrinsic and inherent value is ascribed to ALL of mankind before we were in our mother's womb.* Our identity is wrapped up in the absolute truth of God's character of unconditional love. This is key to understanding our true value and worth. Jesus' desire is that we know who we are in our knowing who He is.

Now let's take a look at the word lost in the familiar context of how religion views mankind's relationship with God. *Being LOST is rarely taught, if ever, in a context of belonging.* In fact it is just the opposite. Within christendom, one spoken of as being in a "lost condition" is one thought to be "outside the fold" or NOT belonging to the family of God. Conditions drive such a mindset. Without acknowledgement of "sonship" / belonging, value becomes a reward for requirements met, ie; confession and repentance of sin, and accepting an invitation given by God. When labeled as lost without value, feelings of worthlessness and rejection take over the mind and heart of the one lost. These feelings are often accompanied by fear of Judgment and condemnation for noncompliance. Religion capitalizes on changing behavior in order to be accepted and find a place of belonging in God's family. Within this context, behavior and performance will continue to be the driving force in one's relationship with God and your value will always be in question. In contrast, when the emphasis is placed on BELONGING there is an entirely different perspective in the mind of both the one lost and the one searching. When acknowledged, the HOPE of being found replaces fear. It can also give rise to a decision to return home, where he belonged all along. We see this demonstrated in the story of the Prodigal Son.

There is much to be gleaned from all 3 parables. I want to spend a little more time on the 3rd parable of the lost son. Our Father God is so beautifully depicted in this story. I truly believe the ABSOLUTE TRUTH of his son's identity is being proclaimed within the Father's decisions and actions despite the son's contradictory behavior. This depicts the INNATE VALUE the Father placed on his son. We also see an inherent sense of belonging within the son which had a profound influence on him while he was estranged. I believe it had an influence on his decision to return home.

120

We do not see the Father running after his son to stop him from leaving, nor his searching day and night as depicted in the other two parables. This is

Being LOST is rarely taught, if ever, in a context of belonging.

significant to me. He may not have physically pursued his son, but he never stopped pursuing him in the interconnectedness of Spirit with his son. They were one.

The Father, well aware of his son's lost condition, gave to him his portion of inheritance when he demanded it. In that culture, asking for his inheritance was equivalent to wishing his Father was dead. The Father went out daily, anticipating his Son's return. He was not willing for his Son to perish, but that he would come to repentance, (a change of mind). When the Son was seen coming toward home, the Father ran toward his Son to embrace him. In my reading and pondering the words prepared and rehearsed in the mind of the son on his journey back home, I can only conclude the following. He had lost his identity. This resulted in foolish choices, giving way to destructive behavior and consequences. I think it's fair to say he had experienced "temporary insanity". The Scripture tells us he "came to his senses", but not without feelings of guilt and shame. As he made his journey to return home, he was in a state of "sin consciousness" mixed with a strong sense of separation from his Father relationally.

It is of great significance to me that the Father did not know the son's intentions when He ran toward his Son that day. He is even reported to have paid little attention to his Son's "rehearsed speech". He interrupted him with unexpected chanting of orders to his hired men. They were to set in motion the celebration which the Father had already prepared in his mind beforehand for his son's anticipated return. The son, while doubting his Father's love, was met with unconditional love.

In summary, the Father's responses throughout this parable were:

- a **Declaration of Sonship and belonging** despite the son's rejection of his father.

- a **Declaration of the Father's will** overshadowing his Son's will.

- a **Declaration of his son's innate and inherent value** despite not knowing his son's motivation for returning.

- a **Declaration of his son's righteousness,** demonstrating the Father entering into his son's guilt and shame, without judgment or condemnation.

Going forward, we cannot ignore the older brother's mindset in this story. He did not know his own value or the value placed on him from within his father's heart and mind. In all reality, he was as lost as his younger brother. He was driven by extrinsic motivation as evidenced in his words to his father in Luke 15:29 (Mirror Study Bible) *"Consider the many years that I have toiled for you like a slave. And at no time did I ever dodge any of your commandments; yet, you never considered rewarding me, even with a little lamb, so I could party with my friends."*

The older brother was as lost as his younger brother.

Within religion, extrinsic value has overshadowed the absolute truth of our innate, inherent and intrinsic value. Within these three parables we see the inexhaustible Love of our Father God. The words within these parables bear testimony to the purpose and intent of Jesus coming to earth as God incarnate in flesh. Jesus demonstrated God's unconditional love and the beautiful life of our design. His love was motivated from within. Please read John 17. Jesus expressed this same love toward all mankind. Knowing who God is and who He declares us to be, gives us our greatest sense of belonging. Trust the Spirit within you. He will always affirm your value, devoid of conditions. That is unconditional Love. Do not take the following Scripture lightly. These are life giving words.

1 Thessalonians 5:19-23 (Mirror Study Bible)
"Do not suffocate the flame of the Spirit within you. The prophetic word is not to be underestimated. Test everything like one would test gold to determine its true value, then treasure that which is precious with great care. Distance yourselves immediately from every practice remotely related to the fruit of the 'I-am-not-tree', which is the typical exhausting law of works system. There, away from any effort of your own, discover how the God of perfect peace who fused you skillfully into oneness – just like a master craftsman would dovetail a carpentry joint – has personally perfected and sanctified the entire harmony of your being without your help! He has restored the detailed default settings. You were re-booted to fully participate in the life of your design, in your spirit, soul and body in blameless innocence in the immediate presence of our Lord Jesus Christ."

God declares you as His own! You are valued and loved! You belong, therefore you will never be truly lost. The only place you will be lost is in your mind. Beware of man made doctrines. Religion teaches that mankind was lost because of Adam. to believe this is to believe a lie. *You were found and declared blameless in Christ before you were ever declared lost and guilty in Adam.* These are words of absolute truth and worthy of

Celebration!

> *Spirit will always affirm your value, devoid of conditions.*

CELEBRATION
OR
CONDEMNATION

From the beginning of time, God has wanted a relationship with mankind that reflects His joy over our being his sons and daughters. (*Zephaniah 3:17b. Amplified Bible Classic Edition ABCE*)

> *He will rejoice over you with joy,*
> *He will rests [in silent satisfaction]*
> *and in His love he will be silent*
> *[and make no mention of past sins,*
> *or even recall them]*
> *He will exult over you with singing."*

In all 3 parables previously discussed, the shepherd, the woman, and the father each initiated CELEBRATION *following the LOST being FOUND.*

In the Story of the Prodigal Son, the older brother was not at all in the mood for Celebrating. His rebellious brother had returned, having broken all the laws. *His mind was focused on condemning not only his brother's*

> *Believing does not make something true. Therefore, unbelief cannot make something untrue.*

behavior, but his Father's as well. Do not miss the significance of this portion of the parable. When we have a distorted view of our Father God, we will have a distorted view of ourself. Why is this important? Because, it will never stop there. We will then see others from that same place of distortion. Value based on performance is counterfeit to the authentic innate, inherent and intrinsic value based on the absolute truth of mankind's origin; identity. This is exactly where the older brother was, in mindset and belief. It is where the church is today. Condemnation always comes on the heels of judgment. These two words are ever present in the minds and hearts of men who have cut their teeth on legalism and never embraced their true identity. Self-righteousness is inevitable yet cleverly disguised when hiding behind indoctrination.

Throughout Scripture, believing is associated with experiencing life. Does this mean unbelief is associated with death? Let's go back to the Father's response to his oldest Son. This is beautifully recorded in The Koinonia Greek New Testament Translation of Luke 15:31-32.

> *"So now the father said to him, O child, you yourself continue being with me always and all my things continue being yours (or: everything [that is] mine is yours). But it continued being binding and necessary to at once be in a good and easy frame of mind (or given thoughts of well-being, cheer and celebration) and to rejoice because this one – your brother – was **existing being dead, and now he comes to life**; and was one having been lost and destroyed – and now he is found."*

How many of us have experienced "existing being dead." Perhaps we have all been there but not realized it. The elder Son certainly didn't. In all reality he was in the same frame of mind as the younger brother. Both did not believe in the unconditional love of their Father and therefore did not live in the security of that love. Did their unbelief negate the

Father's declared love, or deny the position these two boys had as sons? The answer should be a resounding, "NO"! Jesus' words found in John chapter 11 are stunning.

"I Am the resurrection and the life. He who believes in me will live even though he dies. Whoever is alive in the life that I AM will never die."
(vss 25 and 26 Mirror Study Bible)

The effects you attribute to *belief* and *unbelief* will be congruent with your view of God. There is a huge disconnect within doctrines of men with regard to these two words and how they are associated with God's character. When we equate believing with obtaining righteousness as a reward, and unbelief with being unrighteous and receiving judgment and condemnation, believing becomes a condition or requirement under a law of works. It is imperative to understand that truth stands alone. Believing does not make something true. Therefore, unbelief cannot make something untrue.

Believing is being awakened to and embracing absolute truth. Unbelief is living in denial of that truth.

(1 John 2:5 Mirror Study Bible)
"Whoever treasures the logic of God's authentic thought,
has His agape-love (unconditional love) FULLY REALIZED
in its most complete context.
This is what our association and this union in Christ is all about."

Adversarial thoughts foster unbelief and will always be met with truth in our inner man. God IS TRUTH and LOVE. His I AMness is who you are. Even in our unbelief God will always deny our denial of the truth, continuing to declare the truth of our identification in Christ. Who is IN Christ? **ALL** are in Christ and Christ is in **ALL.**

> *God will always deny our denial of the truth.*

Despite what you may have been taught to believe, no decision you made put Him there! When we forget who we are, He enters into our "temporary insanity" and focuses on anticipation of celebration when we come to our senses. God will never focus on anticipated failure with intent to judge and condemn. In the parable discussed in the previous chapter, both sons were unbelievers, but their Unbelief could never invalidate their sonship.

As I bring this chapter to a close, let me say this. There are many who have prayed the sinner's prayer based on a mixed message of fear and love. Though deemed a "believer," they are believing in a god of their own making. The "unbeliever," often seeking the TRUTH, is rejecting the god of the believer because it does not resonate with the Spirit of Christ in them. I thank God for His never ending resolve to show believers and unbelievers alike, His unconditional love. I can only pray that the words spoken in this book will serve as stepping stones in the discovery of your true identity.

(Hebrews 4:10 (Mirror Study Bible)
"God's rest celebrates His finished work; Whoever enters into God's rest
immediately abandons his own efforts to improve what God has already
perfected. The language of the law is 'do'; The language of grace is 'done.' "
(Philippians 4:8 and 9 Mirror Study Bible)
"Now let this be your conclusive reasoning:
consider that which is true about everyone
as evidenced in Christ.
Live overwhelmed by God's opinion of you!
Acquaint yourselves with the revelation of righteousness;
realize God's likeness in you. Make it your business
to declare mankind's redeemed innocence . . .
Study stories that celebrate life."

Celebrate His finished work.

Enter into God's rest.
Rejoice in the truth that
God is always
CELEBRATING YOU!

DISCIPLINE OR PUNISHMENT

"If you don't learn to obey me, you won't learn to obey God." I would often speak these words to my children when they had disobeyed, and correction was imminent. Even today these words are remembered as having significant meaning.

My reaction to their disobedience was rooted in a sincere desire to "train up a child in the way he should go, so even when he is old he will not depart from it." (Proverbs 22:6). It was also clear in Scripture children were to obey their parents. (Ephesians 6:1-3). Our children were very familiar with that verse. Therefore, my expectation for their compliance necessitated some form of punishment in order to be in alignment with God's expectations. Deep down in my heart, my motives were pure.

Looking back, the most detrimental effect of these mindsets and beliefs in my approach to raising my children was the association given to God. I knew no other context. Within Christianity, punishment by parents came in various forms. Proverbs 13:24 and 22:15 were well known verses to support spanking. There is an inborn sense of guilt and shame in all of us when "getting our hand caught in the cookie jar." When fear of punishment becomes the motivation for good behavior, we may see compliance but rarely reformation. It may even encourage ongoing destructive behavior with a "looking over the shoulder" mentality to see if someone is watching while disobedience continues. When God is brought into the equation of surveillance over behavior, and expectation for obedience, it can create a sin conscious mindset. One can become hardened against instruction and correction by parents as well as toward God. My heart's desire was for our 6 children to be obedient to God in order to avoid punishment. But what image of God was I promoting? This fear motivated approach to correction has destroyed many relationships between children and their parents. And for those raised in a religious home, it caused many children to leave the "faith" of their parents. Fear will always bring separation. I have seen it happen over and over again.

(1 John 4:18 Mirror Study Bible)
"Fear cannot co-exist in this love realm. The perfect love union that we are talking about, expels fear. Fear holds on to an expectation of crisis and judgment [which brings separation] and interprets it as due punishment. [a form of cause and effect] It echos torment and only registers in someone who does not yet realize the completeness of their love union [with the Father, Son and Spirit and with one another.]"

So, how does God deal with disobedience? We must first understand what the word obedience means in the original language. The Greek word, "upoakoo" is broken down to "akoo" (to hear) and "upo"(under the influence of). In context here, it is being attentive to or hearing and taking to heart what God believes (His faith) to be true about us and every one in the cosmos, regardless of behavior. Don't miss this. *Disobedience is to default to our own ways and opinions relative to external influences.* We have stopped listening to and embracing God's thoughts toward us.

Take time to read Hebrews chapter 11. It gives the stories of men and women in the Old Testament who lived lives of obedience. Their behavior was not on record as an achievement gaining a reward. Their testimonies were framed in the context of their faith entwined in the faith

To obey is to find a resting place in our oneness and sonship.

of God. They listened to and believed the words of God. They were obedient out of love. Their behavior did not make God's faith happen. They were awakened to faith which was then displayed in their behavior.

From the beginning of time, man has had a choice to obey or disobey. God never made obedience about behavior. Man did. Our mindset on these two words has to become aligned with God's mindset or we will continue to default to behavior. When we default to behavior, fear and condemnation are not far behind. Jesus came to show us the Father's love. He did not come to condemn mankind's behavior. Laws and commandments were never God's idea. Obedience became a platform for self-righteousness. God sees obedience as the awakening to FAITH, in and of God's love. To obey is to find a resting place in our oneness and sonship. Our behavior will automatically reflect His Glory. The author of Hebrews introduces the subject of discipline in chapter 12. This should be kept in context with chapter 11. When I apply critical thinking and logic, I see an important correlation.

(Hebrew 12:6-8 Mirror Study Bible)
"For every instruction (discipline) is inspired by His love ,even as a father would teach His sons with affection, though it might seem harsh at the time. Embrace correction. His instruction confirms your true sonship; Just as a father would take natural responsibility for the education (discipline) of his children. See yourselves as sons, [children of faith], welcoming your spiritual education together with the rest of the family of faith." (described in Hebrews 11)

Punishment and discipline have been used interchangeably throughout History. One might look at their synonymous usage as being inconsequential. I strongly disagree. When these two words are used to describe God's methodology of correcting His children, it is imperative we know their meanings linguistically, and contextually. Rightly dividing and giving correct interpretation to these words is imperative to our having a correct understanding of God's character of love. When we know the absolute truth of the character of God, *Logic tells me that punishment is not in God's vocabulary*, and should never be used when describing His approach to disobedience. In fact, when researching the use of the word punishment, you will find the following substitutions; penalty, justice, judgment, condemned, declared guilty. These words are contradictory to God's character. *When punishment and discipline are used interchangeably, there is the risk of sending a mixed message as to what true love is.* 1 Corinthians 13:5 in any translation tells us that Love keeps no record of wrongs. Our identity is not shaped by our behavior. Our identity is shaped before we were in our Mother's womb. Love is who God is. Love is who we are.

Punishment often becomes about satisfying the accuser who views the accused as less than, unvalued, unloved, unfavored, etc. Discipline focuses on the one being accused, establishing they have value, worth, and are loved. Discipline brings with it the concept of discipleship, leading by example with love rather than demanding compliance with fear. Shepherds of old were an example of this approach. They loved their sheep. They would go before their sheep to lead and guide them away from the potential consequences in wandering. When the sheep went astray, the shepherd sought until he found them. The motive was not to punish but to lovingly discipline them, binding their wounds and carrying them home to safety.

Let me be clear. I am not intimating that there are no consequences for harmful and destructive behavior at any level. Disobedience embodies consequences. When in the cross fires of disobedience, a choice is made with a specific goal in mind; loving discipleship resulting in restoration, or vengeful punishment resulting in retaliation and retribution. The former builds up. The latter tears down.

A highlight in my 40+ years of experience as an RN, was to work in a prison for young men ages 15-24 years of age. Some had committed heinous crimes and were facing long term incarceration. I would weep for these young men. Why? Because they were lost. More than once Jesus referred to mankind as sheep. In Isaiah God tells us that as sheep, we have all gone astray and turned to our own way (Isaiah 53:6). The Scriptures tell us that Jesus had compassion for those who strayed away. These young men were broken and wounded. Many of them were lambs without a shepherd, often raised in fatherless environments and surrounded by physical, emotional and substance abuse. Their behavior was a manifestation of a lost identity. So many of them lacked a sense of belonging, let alone feeling valued. I can only give testimony to the fact that when I treated them with love, and respect, devoid of judgment as to the reason for their incarceration, they responded in kind. I saw Jesus in each one of them. It is God's opinion that defines who we are.

We, like Sheep, need loving leadership, protection, and redirection.

In the Book of Psalms, David speaks of a rod and a staff being used as "tools" of a shepherd. Research confirms that these tools were not used to punish, but rather to protect and redirect in loving discipline. Jesus clearly displayed the character and heart of God in similar fashion. He loves us and disciplines us as a Father would his son or a shepherd would his sheep. We, like Sheep, need loving leadership, protection, and redirection.

Let's look at a Biblical New Testament example of God's loving discipline toward a religious leader named Saul. His personal testimony is recorded in Acts chapter 26:1-18 The Greek New Testament translation is stunning.

Research confirms that Saul was a highly educated man, and a devout pharisee and teacher of the law. Based on Saul's upbringing, he believed that Jesus was an imposter, a blasphemer, and a heretic. Saul truly thought he was serving God by persecuting and sanctioning the murder of many hundreds of jews who followed Jesus claims to be God. How could a religious leader be a murderer, and justify his behavior? It goes back to the question, *Why did he believe what he believed?* It is still not agreed upon by theologians whether or not Paul ever saw or met Jesus face to face. But, there is no dispute that Saul did have a very real encounter with the living God. Scripture tells us that Saul was on the road to Damascus with a mandate issued by the high Priest to arrest all those who followed the teachings of Jesus. They were to be brought back to Jerusalem for questioning with probable execution if they failed to deny the accusations. On that road, Jesus appeared to him in a bright light, causing Saul to be knocked off his horse quite literally, and struck with total blindness. Let's look at the words exchanged in this encounter. Jesus initiated the conversation. *(See Acts 26:14-15a ESV Translation)*

> *"Saul heard a voice in the Hebrew language,*
> *'Saul, Saul, why are you persecuting Me?'*
> *Saul responded with a question,*
> *'Who are you, **Lord**?' "*

Saul's words, though seemingly subservient, clearly indicated that Saul was confused and disoriented. His devotion had been to the law of works. He followed ingrained laws of God, being obedient to the fullest extent of what the law required. This law and performance driven mindset will often go hand in glove with a desire for power. Saul most certainly had developed a thirst for enforcing the laws and controlling people's lives with fear driven motivation. He was certainly on a "high horse" of arrogance. Speaking for myself, I had become blind to my own self righteousness when living a performance driven life, judging myself and others based on behavior.

When we focus on behavior we not only lose sight of our own true identity, but also that of others. Behavior follows mindsets and beliefs. Mindsets

136

and beliefs follow perception of one's identity based on relative truth or absolute truth. *Saul's response was indicative of a lost identity.* He did not know who he was because of his warped view of God from his youth. *Though fully acquainted with words on written scrolls, he was ignorant of THE WORD, JESUS.* He did not believe in a God of unconditional love for him or those he was persecuting. He believed in a judgmental God who demanded obedience and severely punished wrong behavior. Let's look again at this passage and read the words Jesus spoke in response to Saul's inquiry. *(ESV Acts 26:15b)*

> **"I am Jesus** *whom you are persecuting.*
> *But* **rise and stand** *upon your feet,*
> *For* **I have appeared to you for this purpose** *. . . "*

The words of Jesus to Saul are astounding to me and definitely noteworthy. Saul was a murderer. Jesus never brought that up. When or if you read the account for yourself, you will see that Jesus never mentioned his past behavior or reputation. He did not include any condemnation, judgment or wrath toward Saul. In stark contrast, *Jesus was declaring Saul's true God given Identity, value, and place of belonging and purpose.* This is a perfect example of loving discipline, not vengeful punishment. God will never speak to us in words suggestive of a performance driven relationship. He meets us where we are in our self reliance, self centeredness, and self righteousness, reminding us of who He declares us to be and what our purpose is. Paul clearly states this in Galatians 1:16 (Mirror Study Bible).

> *"It pleased the Father to reveal His Son in me*
> *in order that I may proclaim Him in the nations"*

Paul was a son by birthright, not by doing right. It was imperative that Paul knew this before imparting this message of Christ being in all; *not by invitation to become, but as a proclamation of who they were before the foundation of the world.* God's message to Saul is the same message to all mankind today. Jesus declared these words throughout His ministry. I AM, therefore YOU ARE, because . . . IT IS FINISHED! God may, at times, have to knock us off a high horse from time to time in order to remind us of these truths and the value they hold. *(See Hebrews 12:5-7 Mirror Study Bible)* A loving Father knows our needs. His discipline is tailor made for our good and to fulfill God's purpose. Saul certainly did not need a lesson on law or a lecture in doctrine. History tells us that he had studied under Gamaliel, a leading authoritative figure in the sanhedrin council under Roman rule. What Saul needed was a lesson in meekness / humility. Saul, now completely blind, was told to rise and stand. However, he would now need to rely on others to lead him. For a self reliant man, this was a necessary step for Saul to take in this disciplinary process. *Without humility we will not find our true identity.* Without humility our hearing and embracing God's words will be impaired. *Meekness does not infer weakness. Meekness is strength under control.* In this case, Spirit's control. Jesus Himself was meek . . . .but certainly not weak. The opposite of humility is *Self righteousness, which embodies self reliance. In this context self reliance is acting independently and out of character of one's original design.* Jesus said of himself in John 5:19 *(Mirror Study Bible)*

> *"Whatever they see the Son do, Mirrors the Father-*
> *He does not act independent of his Father-*
> *The Son's gaze is fixed in order to accurately interpret*
> *and repeat what He sees His Father do.*
> *The one reveals the other without compromise or distraction."*

This, not behavior, is at the core of obedience. Paul's awakening to His oneness with Christ would empower him to go to those who were blind in their minds and hearts. Saul was God's man, before he was born *(See Galatians 1:15)*. Despite Saul's behavior, God's sovereign plan would not nor could not be thwarted. Jesus will always meet us where we are and equip us for our journey, no matter how difficult the lesson, or how harsh it might seem at the time. *(See Hebrews 12:6)*

Saul received his sight 3 days after his encounter with Jesus. I believe those 3 days of blindness were a strategic part of God's plan. What better object lesson could Jesus have given Saul? His commission was to give the light of the gospel to those who walked in the darkness of their minds. Saul was never abandoned by God when living out of a lost identity. God's method of gaining Saul's attention that day should never be interpreted as punishment for wrong behavior. It was to serve as Saul's "ebenezer", a loving intervention by a loving Father for Saul's good, and God's purpose which was to spread the Gospel. His awareness of God's unconditional love would compel him to keep on keeping on, even in the face of persecucion, near death experiences, and imprisonment. His testimony is well documented in early manuscripts of Scripture. His eternal testimony became, "Once I was blind, but now I can see."

Because of His love, God will never stop disciplining us. He will enter into our blindness on into eternity if need be. I believe with all of my mind and heart that *we were created for an ETERNAL LOVE RELATIONSHIP with our creator. God's mind was made up about our innocence before the foundation of the world.* When God asked Adam, *"Who told you you were naked?"*, and Saul, *"Why are you persecuting me?"*, and the woman, *"Where are your accusers?"*, there was no intent to accuse, condemn, or punish. Jesus spent little to no time discussing Adam's, Saul's, or the Woman's behavior. ie: being naked, a persecutor, or accused adulterer. God's trajectory of thought was aimed straight for their minds and Hearts. His purpose was then, and will always be, to dispel the lies we chose to believe about ourselves and to know who we are as we have always been known by Him *(1 Corinthians 13:12)* and this may require discipline.

It is not clear when God changed Saul's name to Paul. One thing is certain. Paul had spent time with Jesus in solidarity of mind and heart. He found his identity in Christ apart from the law, and fulfilled his purpose by sharing the message of Christ in All. These are his words recorded in Galatians Chapter 1:11,12,17 *(Mirror Study Bible)*. I encourage you to read the entire Book of Galatians to glean from the context.

"I want to make it very clear to you my friends, that the message I proclaim is not mere speculation or the product of philosophical or religious debate. This is not my own invention, neither was I spoon-fed by human tuition; My source of reference is the unveiled mystery of Christ in me. This is radical. I deliberately distanced myself from Jerusalem and the disciples of Jesus."

Identity is who we are, not what we do.

As I was reading this portion of Paul's testimony, I was challenged by God's Spirit to be willing to distance myself from familiar words of men and spend time with Jesus. For Lloyd and me this meant applying critical thinking with logic to what we had been taught for 60+ years. We were asked to leave our brick and mortar church due to our "Road to Emmaus experience." Family and friends do not understand. We choose not to debate. We love with a new found freedom and knowledge that Spirit is the one who opens eyes in His time and His perfect loving ways. We may not have been given a new name like Saul, but we definitely were given a renewed understanding of God's unconditional love free from conditions. We now intentionally love others with this same love. When we began to recognize and acknowledge words contradicting God's character, we embarked upon an incredible journey with THE WORD, Jesus.

*"In your realizing that I am what the Scriptures are all about, you will discover uniquely for yourself, face to face with me, that **you are what I am all about**; and rivers of living waters will gush out of your innermost being."*
(John 7:38 Mirror Study Bible)

Never stop asking yourself why you believe what you believe." Prepare to hear God's voice of affirmation and/or correction. His desire is to show you how wide, long, high, and how deep His love is for YOU! *(see Ephesians 3:18)*

"GO AND SIN NO MORE."

Jesus is acquainted with every word spoken to you, of you, and by you. Words matter to Him, because HE IS THE WORD, the LOGOS of God, and has chosen to live His life in you and through you. When words fill your mind and heart inwardly or outwardly, they are met with the very Spirit of God, and weighed in the balance with words of ABSOLUTE TRUTH. This final chapter brings us back to the beginning. Words matter, because you matter. The exchange of words recorded in John 8:1-11 resonated with my Spirit and has changed me forever. Where are your accusers?, is one of two questions asked by Jesus of an unnamed woman allegedly caught in the act of adultery. After meditating on this portion of Scripture, I have concluded that this woman is a representation of all mankind. I say with purpose and intent that Jesus will never grow weary of asking us, "Where are your accusers?" and "Has no one condemned you?" He will then wait patiently, with celebratory anticipation, for us to respond as this woman did. *"No one Lord."*

Why are these questions and her response significant? Every day we are faced with words of accusation in some level of communication.

I make that statement based on the fact that accusations are rooted in expectations. When a behavior does not meet an expectation, an accusation is not far behind in the thought process and/or impending exchange of words inwardly or outwardly. A verdict of innocence or guilt becomes a choice made by the accuser and the accused. All behavior has consequences as discussed in a previous chapter. But, addressing consequences based on expectations is treating symptoms and ignoring the disease. Identity is who we are, not what we do. Who we are is absolute. What we do is relative to our perceptions of what we believe to be true about ourselves. Awakening to the truth of our Identity allows us to separate adversarial words of accusation, from God's words of affirmation. The former focuses on our guilt. The latter focuses on our declared innocence.

Jesus knew the thoughts and intents of the hearts of all involved in this story recorded in John 8:1-11;

- The Religious leaders
- The surrounding crowd of people
- The woman

The Religious leaders clearly focussed on the law. Their motives were to align behavior with the law using fear of punishment to force compliance. Jesus' focus was and will always be; to remind us of who God says we are so we can align our thoughts with His thoughts, despite our behavior. All involved or witnessing this encounter were presented with two opposing mindsets; legalism rooted in unbelief and rest rooted in God's finished work in creation and fully demonstrated in the finished work of Christ on the cross. The author of Hebrews understood this dichotomy. More importantly . . . so did Jesus. Let us examine the closing words spoken by Jesus to the woman accused.

"Go and sin no more."

"Faith (not willpower) realizes our immediate access into God's rest."

At face value It would seem that Jesus did have something to say about this woman's behavior. After all, He used the word "*SIN*." Wouldn't this word be referring back to her alleged act of adultery? For decades I believed that Jesus was saying, "Go . . . and don't commit adultery again." This would seem to be contradictory to His previous words indicating He found no fault in her. Could these words be considered words of warning? Was Jesus intimating that she was forgiven this time, but He may not come to her defense the next time? Or worse yet, was Jesus saying to make this wrong choice again, she might forfeit His forgiveness for all eternity? I have never heard these thoughts of mine verbalized from a pulpit. But, based on the doctrine I was taught, the word "*SIN*" *was* always equated to disobedience to God's word . . . the Bible. In fact, the attention given to these words of Jesus within the context / mindset inferred above, seemed to overshadow His words of acquittal and unconditional love. I always came away with a mixed message. Within his words of forgiveness for my disobedience will be words of warning, not to do it again, leaving me some element of fear. Because everyone identifies more with the struggles of bad behavior than a declared innocence, we often leave with sin consciousness. We climb back onto the hamster wheel of trying harder NOT to do whatever it is we struggle with. According to the author of Hebrews this is unbelief; choosing not to enter into God's rest.

> "Faith (not willpower) realizes our immediate access
> into God's rest.
> Hear the echo of God's cry through the ages,
> 'Oh if only they would enter into my rest.'
> His rest celebrates perfection. His work is complete;
> The fall of mankind did not flaw its perfection."
> *(Hebrews 4:3 Mirror Study Bible)*

In my sojourn with words, as previously expressed, I became aware of the crucial need for a linguistic, cultural, historical, and contextual approach to receiving words; most assuredly from within the pages of Scripture. Without such, accuracy in interpretation and understanding of the deliverer's purpose and intent is compromised; Applying these principles to the words Jesus spoke in this Biblical account, entwined with the Spirit of God, literally brought a depth of understanding and rest to my soul.

The prodigal son chose to live a life inferior to what was his from birth.

One of the most misunderstood and misinterpreted words in our English translations of the Bible is the word *SIN*. I see it as one of the most important words in all of Scripture. By including the following definition of words, I pray it will motivate you to go beyond familiar words on a page and find hidden treasures of truth. The Greek word for **SIN** is **Hamartia.** When translated, the word is broken down into two parts. *Ha,* meaning negative or without, and *meros,* meaning portion or form; therefore **without form.** When examining the word Sin as defined above, and the word transformed used in 2 Corinthians 3:18, there is contrast with correlation. **Transformed** in the Greek is **metamorpho.** Meta means together with. Morphe means form; therefore **with form.** This is the opposite of hamartia-without form or in other words, distorted form. *"Hamartia suggests anything that could possibly distract from the awareness of our likeness. Sin is to live out of context with the blueprint of one's design; to behave out of tune with God's original harmony."* (Francois du Toit commentary note on John 8:11 and also in John 5:14 and Commentary note 2 Corinthians 3:18 Mirror Study Bible) It is amazing to me how every word study book I own, every Concordance specifically written for each translation of the Bible, gives the definition for Hamartia as "MISSING THE MARK". Although I cannot argue with this definition, it is incomplete. Romans 3:23 is a commonly memorized verse in Scripture where the word sin is interpreted in this way. *"For all have sinned (missed the mark) and fall short of the Glory of God"* (Romans 3:23 ESV) However, I would take issue with the fact that these word study guides have taken this interpretation of

146

the word sin, and placed a strong emphasis on, and binding connection to wrong behavior. "Missing the mark" becomes disobedience to God's commands with little to no mention of the root meaning, without form or identity. Please note that this verse does not say, fall short of the behavior of God. Though most of us are familiar with the phrase, "What would Jesus do?, it should never be applied to this verse.

Moving on, have you ever asked yourself what "fall short" means or what "the Glory of God" is? ***Hustereo*** in Greek is to fall short. Its meaning is ***"to be inferior".*** Now let's look at the whole thought portrayed here when linked with God's Glory. ***Doxa*** is the Greek word for ***Glory***, blueprint, from ***dokeo*** meaning ***opinion or intent***. Glory is also associated with celebration and praise. God's opinion and intent is best displayed in Jesus. He lived life in absolute ONENESS with His Father. *Jesus knew who He was and lived out of "I AM" not out of "I Do."*

The prodigal son chose to live a life inferior to what was his from birth. When he "came to his senses" and awakened to the reality of his sonship, he entered into celebration with His Father. From God's point of view, our identity is never in question, but can and will be challenged. Even Jesus, God in flesh, was challenged in the wilderness to act independently of His Father. Jesus chose to go through the wilderness in the awareness of His oneness with God, thus displaying God's purpose and intent for Him on this earth. His life was an example of us and for us. We were made in His image and likeness to display the blueprint of God's Glory. You can read this account in Matthew chapter 4:1-11. He focused on the message He was sent to proclaim to the entire human race. The following words spoken by Jesus to His Father become our focus when we awaken to our true identity.

"I am in them as you are in me, and on this basis
their seamless oneness may be entirely concluded"
And I have made the essence of your being
known to them so that they may know you by name;

And I will also give them understanding
to know that the same love wherewith you have loved me
is in them even as I am in them."
(John 17:23, 26 Mirror Study Bible)

When our relationship with God is NOT focused on God's unconditional love, we will continue to live in an inferior mindset driven by our own self righteous behavior. The perception of our identity needs to change. Our mind needs to be renewed. This is exactly what Jesus was accomplishing in His encounter with the woman. Jesus came to show us the Father's unconditional love by revealing to us our identity, devoid of behavioral requirements. Jesus was fully aware of this woman's behavior. He also knew the behavior of each one of the accusing religious teachers of the law. His words written in the sand and spoken outright to them, gave evidence of the power of God's words. They threw down their stones and left the scene. Their identity had been challenged by the one who knew them completely. There was no recorded evidence of their choosing to acknowledge the truth in His words. They walked away, continuing to live under the law of works. May we never forget that in just a short time after this recorded encounter above, Jesus declared His unconditional LOVE by willingly going to the cross, and died for those teachers of the law, the woman, and all who witnessed the event. When my husband, Lloyd, shouted YES!, from the banks of the Rogue River that day, he was spot on. Jesus did die for the whole world. He died for all, as all, and is in all. Jesus knew this woman's deepest need was to be reminded of who she was and who she belonged to. Is this not true of all of us? All are the innocent lamb that had gone astray, the lost coin of value, the 2 sons who had denied their Father's love. (see Luke 15)

Have you ever wondered why Jesus asked this woman these 2 questions? He could have turned His attention to her and the crowd and declare her acquittal with a command to go and sin no more. Once again I see the Father's purpose and intent. Jesus desired her participation in and acknowledgment of truth. Why? Jesus knew that *words of truth spoken from her lips would not only validate His unconditional love for her, but also align her thoughts with His thoughts and her words with His words.* God's desire was for her to *know herself as she had always been fully known by Him before the beginning of time.* This exchange of words was not only for her benefit, but also for the crowd of witnesses in the temple square. Her testimony was one of courage and faith. God's faith became her faith. His declaration of innocence became her belief. She was free from accusation and condemnation based on her identity, not her behavior. She entered into His rest.

Dare to throw years of familiar words into the Wind of God's Spirit. The chaff of chastisement will blow away and you will be left with the pure grain of His Grace. Every word of God matters because you matter. When Jesus asks you, **"Where are Your Accusers? Has no one condemned you?"** Boldly respond, **"No one, Lord."** Then believe what He declares you and everyone in the cosmos to be before the foundation of the world for all eternity . . . **Not guilty!**

"Now the decisive conclusion is this;
In Christ,
every bit of condemning evidence against us is canceled"
(Romans 8:1 Mirror Study Bible)

Go and believe what God Believes to be true about YOU!

The Gospel, CHRIST IN ALL, is confirmed when examining the following Scriptures. The list below is shared with expressed permission, from the Why Guy's Book, "In Defense of God's Love." Translations used were not indicated but, let me assure you of this fact. ALL means ALL in any language.

Genesis 12:3 "ALL peoples on earth will be blessed through Abraham."

Genesis 22:18 "ALL nations on earth will be blessed through Abraham's offspring."

Psalm 22:27   "ALL the ends of the earth and ALL the families of the nations will acknowledge God."

Psalm 33:15 "God Fashions ALL hearts."

Psalm 65:2   "To You (God) ALL flesh shall come."

Psalm 86:9   "ALL nations will worship Him."

Psalm 145:9-10   "The Lord has compassion on ALL His creation and ALL He has made will praise Him."

Psalm 145: 13-14   "The Lord loves ALL His creation. He raises ALL WHO FALL." (even back sliders)

Samuel 14:14   "We must ALL die; we are like water spilled on the ground, which cannot be gathered up. But God will NOT take away a life; He will devise plans so as NOT TO KEEP AN OUTCAST BANISHED FOREVER FROM HIS PRESENCE."

Isaiah 25:6-8   "God will prepare a feast for ALL PEOPLE, He will destroy the shroud that enfolds ALL peoples, the sheet that covers up ALL nations. He will eliminate death, wipe away the tears from ALL FACES and remove the disgrace of his people from all the earth."

Isaiah 45:22-23   "God has sworn an oath that (ALL) EVERY knee will bow before Him and every tongue will swear by Him."

Isaiah 49:6   "God's salvation will be brought to the ends of the earth."

Jeremiah 31:33-34   "ALL men will know God, from the greatest to the least."

Matthew 18:13   "Like the man who owns a hundred sheep and is not willing to lose even one, God is not willing that any one be lost."

Luke 2:10   "The birth of Jesus is good news for ALL the people."

Luke 3:6   "ALL flesh shall see God's salvation."

Luke 15:4   "If ANY (ALL) stray He goes after that which is lost until He finds it."

John 1:29   "Jesus is the Lamb of God who takes away the sin of the WORLD."

John 3:35   "The Father has given ALL into His hands."

John 4:42   "Jesus is Savior of the WORLD."

John 5:25   "Even the dead will hear the sound of Christ and ALL who hear will live."

John 5:28   "ALL in the grave will hear and come forth."

John 6:37   "Everything (ALL) that God has given to Christ will come to Him."

John 6:39   "This is the will of the Father who sent me, that of ALL He has given Me, I SHOULD LOSE NOTHING, but raise them up at the last day."

John 12:32   "Jesus will draw ALL mankind unto Himself."

John 12:47   "I do not judge ANYONE who hears my words and does not keep them, for I CAME NOT TO JUDGE THE WORLD, BUT TO SAVE THE WORLD."

John 17:2   "He (Jesus) has authority over ALL flesh to give eternal life."

Acts 3:20 (Restitution of ALL) And that He may send [to you] the Christ (the Messiah), who before was designated and appointed for you.. even Jesus, Whom heaven must receive [and retain] until the time for the complete (universal) RESTORATION OF ALL that God spoke by the mouth of all His Holy prophets for ages past [from the most ancient time in the memory of man.]"

Romans 3:3-4   "The unbelief of some will not nullify God's faithfulness."

Romans 5:15   "In Adam ALL condemned, in Christ ALL live."

Romans 5:18   "Therefore just as one man's trespass led to condemnation for ALL, so one man's act of righteousness leads to justification and life for ALL."

Romans 8:38-39   "Nothing can separate us from the love of God that is in Christ."

Romans 11:15   "Reconciliation of the WORLD"

Romans 11:32 "He has shut ALL up in unbelief to show mercy to ALL."

1 Corinthians 3:15 "ALL saved, so as by fire"

1 Corinthians 15:22 "In Adam ALL die, in Christ ALL live."

2 Corinthians 5:15 "Jesus died for ALL."

2 Corinthians 5:19 "Through Christ, God was reconciling the WORLD (ALL) to Himself."

Ephesians 1:10-11 "ALL come into Him at the fullness of times. God will bring ALL things under heaven and on earth under Christ."

Ephesians 1:22 "Therefore He has put ALL things in subjection to Christ."

Ephesians 4:10 "Christ ascended higher than all heavens to fill the WHOLE (ALL) universe."

Philippians 2:11 "Every (ALL) tongue will confess that Jesus is Lord."

Colossians 1:20 "ALL reconciled unto God"

1 Timothy 2:4 "God will have ALL to be saved and ALL to come to the knowledge of truth."

1 Timothy 2:6 "Salvation of ALL is testified in due time."

1 Timothy 4:10 "God is the Savior of ALL men, expeciall (not exclusively) those who believe."

Titus 2:11-12 "God's grace, which brings salvation has appeared to ALL men."

Hebrews 2:9   "Jesus tasted death for everyone (ALL)."

Hebrews 7:25   "Jesus is able to save to the UTTERMOST."

Hebrews 8:11   "ALL will know God."

2 Peter 3:9   "ALL come to repentance"

1 John 2:2   "And He is the atoning sacrifice for our (believers) sins, and NOT OURS ONLY, but ALSO FOR THE SINS OF THE WHOLE WORLD."

1 John 4:14   "Christ is the Savior of the WORLD" (ALL)

Revelation 5:13   "Every (ALL) creature in heaven on earth, under the earth, and on the sea will sing praises to Him who sits on the throne and to the Lamb (Christ)."

Revelation 21:4-5 . . . "God will dwell with men and He will wipe every (ALL) tears from their eyes, death, mourning, crying, pain and the old order of things will pass and everything will be made new."

Special Thanks

It is with the deepest respect and admiration I thank my Editor, Julianna Forgione. God knew exactly who and what I needed when He gave me YOU! Your patience and perseverance through multiple rewrites deserves a medal. We became "one" as we navigated the seas of uncharted waters. Thank you for many hours of wise counsel along my arduous journey. Truly your efforts were a labor of love. I could not have accomplished this task without you. You are more than an editor. I am proud to call you my friend. You're the "bestest." www.justjulianna.com DBA Belief Relief

To Alexa Weisman AKA "granddaughter." Your involvement and support during those early days of writing could only be surpassed by your loving encouragement to keep writing the truth, no matter the repercussions. With your God given talents and gifts, you took the desires of my heart and began the process of putting ink on paper. You were and continue to be an inspiration to me. Thank you for believing in me. www.honeybook.com

To Deborah Perdue, Illumination Graphics. God's timing is perfect. When words ceased to fly, needing a place to land, you appeared. You have illustrated my purpose and intent with accuracy and precision. Your graphic design and formatting skills transformed invisible ideas and dreams into visible realities. You are truly the final stroke of the brush on the canvas of my mind. I will be forever grateful, thanks. www.illuminationgraphics.com